William Chambers

American slavery and colour

William Chambers

American slavery and colour

ISBN/EAN: 9783744741743

Printed in Europe, USA, Canada, Australia, Japan

Cover: Foto ©ninafisch / pixelio.de

More available books at **www.hansebooks.com**

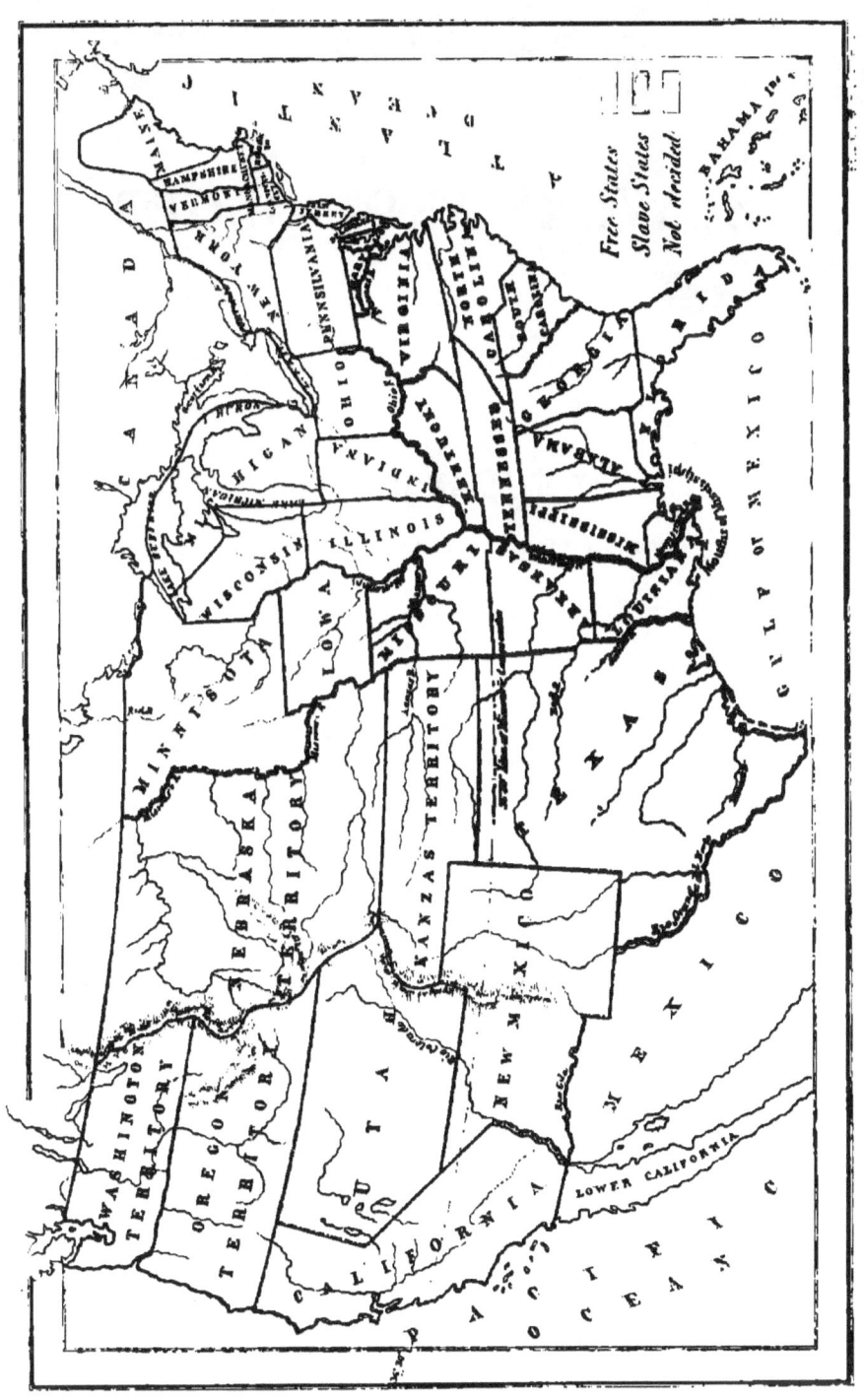

AMERICAN

SLAVERY AND COLOUR

BY WILLIAM CHAMBERS
AUTHOR OF 'THINGS AS THEY ARE IN AMERICA'

LONDON
W. & R. CHAMBERS, PATERNOSTER ROW
AND DIX AND EDWARDS, NEW YORK
1861

The sight of a few Slave Sales has a wonderful effect in awakening the feelings on the subject of Slavery. The thing is seen to be an undeniable reality—no mere invention of the novelist. From time to time, the spectacle of an auction-stand on which one man is selling another, flashes back upon the mind. For three years, I have been haunted by recollections of that saddening scene, and taken a gradually deepening interest in American Slavery—its present condition, its mysterious future. Having already referred to the subject, I should not again have intruded on public notice, but for the recent exciting discussions concerning Slavery, the protracted struggle in Kansas, and the probability of further contests between Slavery and Freedom, consequent on the organisation of new States in the southern section of the Union.

The present volume, tracing the progress of Slavery, and presenting such other particulars as may afford a comprehensive view of the subject, is offered as a small contribution to a department of literature daily increasing in interest—an expression of sympathy from an unenrolled adherent of a great and sacred cause.

March 1857.

Since this work was issued in 1857, important events, bearing on the subject of Slavery, have occurred in the United States. These matters are referred to in a Postscript and the Appendix, and the volume may therefore be said to complete the historical sketch of American Slavery until the present time.

W. C.

EDINBURGH, *June* 1861.

AMERICAN SLAVERY AND COLOUR.

SOUTHERN DEMONSTRATIONS.

'RACE! Do not speak to us of race—we care nothing for breed or colour. What we contend for is, that slavery, whether of black or white, is a normal, a proper institution in society.' So proclaim southern writers in the United States. The principle of enslaving only coloured persons, descendants of imported Africans, is now antiquated, and a scheme which embraces slavery of every race and variety of complexion is at length put forward as a natural and desirable arrangement for all parties—a highly commendable state of things. Any one could have foreseen that it must come to this. The prodigious and irregular amalgamation of races in the south, with the deterioration and helplessness of the less-affluent class of whites in the slaveholding states, has, as may be supposed, led to a pretty nearly pure, nay, absolutely pure breed of white slaves. A new style of reasoning is consequently required. If slavery is to be at all vindicated, it must not now be on the narrow basis of colour, but on the broad grounds, that there is an inherent right in the stronger and more wealthy classes to reduce the poorer, and, it may be, more ignorant orders to a state of perpetual bondage. The cool announcement of this extraordinary doctrine, from influential parties in a great thriving republic, strikes one with so much wonder, that we almost inquire if we have heard aright, or if we are really living in the second half of the nineteenth century.

The most casual glance at the products of the southern press leaves no room for doubt on the subject. A few scraps cannot but be classed among the curiosities of modern literature. Mr Fitzhugh, a southern writer, says: 'We do not adopt the theory that Ham was the ancestor of the negro race. The Jewish slaves were not negroes, and to confine the justification of slavery to that of race, would be to weaken the Scriptural authority, and to lose the whole weight of profane authority; for we read of no negro slavery in ancient times. Slavery, black or white, is right and necessary.' The *Richmond Inquirer*, an able Virginian paper, says: 'Until recently, the defence of slavery has laboured under great difficulties, because its apologists—for they were mere apologists—took half-way grounds. They confined the defence of slavery to mere negro slavery; thereby giving up the slavery principle, admitting other forms of slavery to be wrong. The line of defence is now changed. The south now maintains that slavery is right, natural, and necessary. While it is far more obvious that negroes should be slaves than whites—for they are only fit to labour, not to direct—yet the principle of slavery is itself right, and does not depend on difference of complexion.'

Mr G. W. Weston, a writer in the cause of emancipation in the *New York Tribune*, observes: 'It is not true, in law or in fact, that the condition of slavery at the south is confined to the African race. The principle of American slavery which distinguishes it from the slavery of patriarchal times, and from oriental slavery at this day, is, that where the mother is enslaved, the offspring follow the condition of the mother. The female slaves, exposed of necessity to the disorderly passions of the whites, are made the instruments through whom the Caucasian race is itself reduced to the condition of servitude. The blood of orators, statesmen, generals, and even presidents, flows in the veins of thousands who are bought and sold like mules and horses. The time is not distant when the genuine unmixed African will not be found at the south. He is already rare, although it is less than half a century since the prohibition of the foreign slave-trade.' Besides the source of whiteness above referred to, it is understood that numbers of purely Anglo-American children pass into slavery. In some instances, the indigent whites of the south sell their children to traders; and the practice of kidnapping white children in the northern states, and transferring them southward, is said to be notoriously on the increase. We see it mentioned that, in the city of New York alone, as many as thirty children on an average are stolen yearly; it being shrewdly guessed that many of them are carried to the markets of the south, where a good price for them can be readily obtained. If there be the slightest truth in the supposition that gently nurtured white infants are so abstracted from the homes of their parents, nothing could give a more forcible impression of the horrors entailed on American society by the tolerance of slavery within its bosom.

It has been customary to blame England for having, in the first instance, introduced negro slavery into the States; but, admitting to its full extent her guilt in the slave-trade, we can hardly see how her doings in this respect are to be consistently condemned, if American writers be sincere in thinking that slavery is a normal and absolutely necessary institution. From the sentiments lately avowed, it would appear that there can be no right condition of affairs without slaves. Free labour is spoken of as improper, and a thing that must end in national disaster. The only security is for every man who has the means to buy slaves, and get all his work done by them. A widely circulated newspaper—the *New Orleans Delta*—says: 'We have a proposition to lay down that may appear startling to many because it is new, but will have weight and consideration with the thinking, inasmuch as it is based on both philosophy and experience. We therefore declare that slavery is not only national in its origin, but it is essential to republican nationality. But for slavery, republicanism would have long since become a tale in these United States. It is among the slaveholding population that republicanism has had its true home and only defence. It is they who have made the Union what it is commercially and politically. It is only they who can hereafter maintain a safe and honourable union, and enjoy rational liberty. History is instructive; heed its teachings; they are invariable and unerring. It tells us that a great republic never existed without slavery. It tells us that where partial and defined slavery did not exist of law, the mass of the working-people have been slaves, and worse than slaves. It tells us that wherever universal freedom has nominally existed, poverty, want, and possible famine, and humiliating dependency of the poor on the rich, have been the price of painted delusion. Slavery was an institution in all the ancient republics, but in two we have eminent examples. In Rome, the mightiest in arms, and Athens, the most glorious in art of all the old republics, slavery prevailed to a greater extent than in any state of the Union. In Athens, the proportion of slaves to freemen was about two to one—in Rome, scarcely less; and yet with this institution imbedded in their very hearts, they lived and flourished, century after century, and reached a magnificence and grandeur of which the history of modern free society affords no example. Modern free society, as at present organised, is radically wrong and rotten. It is self-destroying, and can never exist happily and normally until it is qualified by the introduction of some principle equivalent in effect to the institution of negro slavery. In the northern states, free society has proved a failure. It is rotten to the core. Let the dominion which its putrescence has engendered succeed, and society, with its most sacred sanctions and its holiest institutions, will fall before it, both in the north and south, and the country must become the seat of howling anarchy or iron despotism. Negro slavery, then, is the conservative element of republicanism, and the firmest basis of society in these United States. Such being the social and political value of slavery, its diffusion and extension are of the first importance, and nothing at the present time should more nearly interest the wise philanthropist and the patriotic statesman, than to devise measures to effect these objects—to restore slavery to its original national character, and make it an object of political solicitude.'

These notions are far from singular. By several writers, freedom is spoken of with coarse contempt. 'Free society!' says the *Muscogee Herald*, an Alabama newspaper. 'We sicken at the name. What is it but a conglomeration of greasy mechanics, filthy operatives, small-fisted farmers, and moon-struck theorists? All the northern, and especially the New England States, are devoid of society fitted for well-bred gentlemen. The prevailing class one meets with is that of mechanics struggling to be genteel, and small farmers who do their own drudgery, and yet who are hardly fit for association with a southern gentleman's body-servant. This is your free society, which the northern hordes are endeavouring to extend into Kansas.' It would be unjust to lay too much stress on the grotesque ravings of an obscure print, did they not find an echo in the *Richmond Inquirer*, a paper which, as already hinted, is conducted with no mean ability. 'Repeatedly,' says its editor, 'have we asked the north—Has not the experiment of universal liberty failed? Are not the evils of free society insufferable? and do not most thinking men among you propose to subvert and reconstruct it? Still no answer. This gloomy silence is another conclusive proof, added to many other conclusive evidences we have furnished, that free society in the long-run is an impracticable form of society; it is everywhere starving, demoralised, and insurrectionary. We repeat, then, that policy and humanity alike forbid the extension of the evils of free society to new people and coming generations. Two opposite and conflicting forms of society cannot, among civilised men, co-exist and endure. The one must give way, and cease to exist; the other become universal. If free society be unnatural, immoral, unchristian, it must fall, and give way to slave society —a social system, old as the world, universal as man.' It would seem that the measure of public liberty which Washington fought for and achieved, is a blunder; and that for the much-venerated free institutions of the States, must be substituted the mixture of aristocracy and helotism of the ancient world.

Another Virginian print, the *Richmond Examiner*, about two years ago came out with a flat contradiction of there being any longer a desire to see the country clear of slavery. 'It is all a hallucination to suppose that we are ever going to get rid of African slavery, or that it will ever be desirable to do so. It is a thing that we cannot do without—that is *righteous, profitable,* and permanent, and that belongs to southern society as inherently, intricately, and durably as the white race itself. Yea, the white race will itself emigrate from the southern states to Africa, California, or Polynesia, sooner than the African. Let us make up our minds, therefore, to put up with and make the most of the institution. Let us not bother our brains about what *Providence* intends to do with our negroes in the distant future, but glory in and profit to the utmost by what He has done for them in transplanting them here and setting them to work on our plantations. Let the politicians and planters of the south, while encouraging the "Baptists and Methodists" —and other denominations having a less number of votes—in Christianising the negro, keep their slaves at hard work, under strict discipline, out of idleness and mischief, while they live; and when they come to die, instead of sending them off to Africa, or manumitting them to a life of "freedom," licentiousness, and nuisance, will them over to their children, or direct them to be sold where they will be made to work hard, and be of service to their masters and to the country. True philanthropy to the negro begins, like charity, at home; and if southern men would act as if the canopy of heaven were inscribed with a covenant, in letters of fire, that *the negro is here, and here for ever; is our property, and ours for ever; is never to be emancipated; is to be kept hard at work, and in rigid subjection all his days*; and is never to go to Africa, to Polynesia, or to Yankee Land—far worse than either—they would accomplish more good for the race in five years than they boast the institution itself to have accomplished in two centuries, and cut up by the roots a set of evils and fallacies that threaten to drive the white race a-wandering in the western wilderness, sooner than Cuffee will go to preach the gospel in Guinea.'

We should imagine that to most of our readers these sentiments will come with startling novelty. While the philanthropists of England are contriving all kinds of meliorations in social economy, they do not appear to be aware that in the progress of events beyond the Atlantic, views have arisen respecting the slave question which are altogether obstructive of popular freedom, and calculated to reduce every unprotected labourer to the condition of a chattel. 'We have,' says the *South-side Democrat*, a Virginian contemporary of the *Inquirer*—' we have got to hating everything with the prefix *free*, from free negroes down and up through the whole catalogue—free farms, free labour, free society, free will, free thinking, free children, and free schools. But the worst of all these abominations is the modern system of free schools.' The only relief can arise from a return to that blessed state in which the bulk of the population shall be kept in ignorance and servitude under a strong-handed minority—there is, it is alleged, no other means to assuage the poverty incidental to universal competition. All who are unable to maintain their families in decency, had better be at once sold to those who are disposed to take charge of them. 'Sell the parents of these children into slavery. Let our legislature (continues the authority just quoted) pass a law, that whoever will take these parents, and take care of them and their offspring, in sickness and in health, clothe them, feed them, and house them, shall be legally entitled to their services; and let the same legislature decree, that whoever receives these parents and their children, and obtains their services, shall take care of them as long as they live.' We infer from all that is told of the condition of the impoverished 'white trash' in the southern states, that the legislative measures here pointed at would present a natural and not unlikely solution of a somewhat puzzling question. Sanguine as are our expectations of social advancement, under prudent safeguards, who can tell that at least a section of a great nation may not, even in our times, return to the almost forgotten usages of medieval Europe. The world is after all, perhaps, not so vastly improved as one would be inclined to think.

Unlike the serfdom of the middle ages, when war and famine carried off no small share of the redundant population, southern slavery cannot be successfully maintained unless means be found for employing the increase on adjoining lands, or disposing of it for transit to distant settlements. The pressing necessity for extending limited properties into large possessions, is stated to be operating on a gigantic scale in Alabama. The Hon. C. C. Clay, Jun., on lately addressing a Horticultural Society in that great cotton-growing state, laments the absorption of small properties. 'Our wealthier planters,' he observes, 'with greater means, and no more skill, are buying out their poorer neighbours, extending their plantations, and adding to their slave force. Of the 20,000,000 of dollars annually realised from the sales of cotton crop of Alabama, nearly all not expended in supporting the producers is reinvested in land and negroes. Thus, the white population has decreased, and the slave increased, almost *pari passu* in several counties in our state. In 1825, Madison county cast about 3000 votes; now she cannot exceed 2300. In traversing that county, one will discover numerous farmhouses, once the abode of industrious and intelligent freemen, now occupied by slaves, or tenantless, deserted, and dilapidated; he will observe fields once fertile, now unfenced, abandoned; he will see the moss growing on the mouldering walls of once thrifty villages, and will find "one only master grasps the whole domain," that once furnished happy homes for a dozen white families.' To this dismal description, that respectable authority, Olmsted, says that the political experiment of Old Virginia, the Carolinas, and Georgia, is being repeated to the same fatal result in Young Alabama.

The generally blighting influence of slavery is clearly a main cause of its extension. To exist at all, it must push into new regions, everywhere exhausting lands, extinguishing freedom, and dishonouring independent rural industry. Pursued by a fearful Nemesis, the slave-power still seeks for more and more scope for its devastating encroachments. An amount of labour far beyond the bounds of internal supply is in demand. If the great west is to be added piecemeal to the slave states of the Union, the breeding establishments of Virginia will fail to furnish stock except at exorbitant prices. Nothing, accordingly, remains but a legalised revival of the slave-traffic from the coast of Africa, or the legal extension of slavery to the poorer classes of the white population. We have seen what is said of the latter expedient; and a desire to supply the labour-market by the former odious means, is likewise expressed in no reserved terms. The *New Orleans Delta* says, on a late occasion, 'We not only desire to make territories, now free, slave territories, and to acquire new territory into which to extend slavery—such as Cuba, North-eastern Mexico, &c.—but we would reopen the African slave-trade, that every white man might have a chance to make himself owner of one or more negroes, and go with them and their household gods wherever opportunity beckoned to enterprise. But the North would never consent to this; they would dissolve the Union rather than grant it, say the croaking impracticables. Gentlemen, you do not know the North, oracular as you look when dubiously shaking your heads. It would not oppose any more bitterly a large demand like this, boldly made, than the smallest one, faintly and politely urged. Try it. There is nothing to lose by the experiment. At all events, if the attempt to reopen this trade should fail, it would give one more proof of how injurious our connection with the North has become to us, and would indicate one more signal advantage which a southern confederacy would have over the present heterogeneous association called the Union.' How the North has deserved that cut! The advantages of a revived African slave-trade were argumentatively pointed out by the *Charleston Standard* so recently as last October. 'From first to last, there has been a constant want of labour. Three millions of our people have perhaps as many slaves as they naturally require; but there are three millions more who are unsupplied. They would take slaves if they could get them; but they are not to be had at prices which will enable them to be used in competition with the free labour of the world. All we have are wanted for agriculture, and even these are not enough. While all are employed, and employed most profitably, lands all over the country are parched and unprofitable, for the want of labour, and millions more could have been absorbed. The labour of those brought one year, would have paid for those to be brought the next; as employments opened, white men of enterprise would have come in more abundance than they have done; the stream of labour from Africa would have met a stream of enterprise from Europe; both would have poured in together; the population of the southern states would have been more dense; the population of the northern states would have been more sparse; Georgia would have been to New York as New York is now to Georgia; other states from Texas and New Mexico would have been brought in; and thus, if the slave states had held on to the sources of their real power, the South would have been the Union. . . . . There is now buried under every acre of land in South Carolina at least fifty dollars in gold; and the day that the savage African is landed on our shores to cultivate it, that gold will glitter on its surface.'

It will not be imagined that these wild opinions meet with universal response in the South, where, indeed, many planters above the ordinary standard are conscious of the evils of slavery, and would gladly listen to any reasonable plan for relieving themselves of their coloured dependents. Least of all do such notions meet with approval in the North. But it is not less certain that, from causes not far to seek, a new tone of sentiment has begun to prevail among the general slaveholding interest. What was long lamented and reluctantly endured, is now resolutely maintained, and arguments are found to vindicate its indefinite extension. A high civil functionary, Mr Adams, governor of South Carolina, in his late message to the legislature of that state, goes quite as far a length as any of the newspapers above quoted. Referring to the pressure against slavery, he speaks of the necessity for prompt measures to fortify and extend it. He recommends the passage of a law exempting from legal seizure and sale, at least one slave; so that every family of whites may be stimulated to possess property 'in some degree above the casualties of debt.' Referring to the increasing demand for slaves to cultivate cotton, he sees no other means for retaining a monopoly in producing that article, than the importation of slaves. Cheap labour must be obtained, and this can be done only in one way—by reopening the African slave-trade. What followed, we give in Mr Adams's own words:

'Until Providence interposes and changes his organism, the African must continue to be a "hewer of wood and drawer of water." It is a diseased sentimentality which starts back at the idea of legalising the slave-trade, and, at the same time, contemplates without emotion the cruel servitude which capital exacts of labour, all the world over. There was a time when canting philanthropists had instilled into us a belief that slavery was wrong. Investigation has entirely changed the once common sentiment on this point. The South now believes that a mysterious Providence has brought the two races together on this continent for wise purposes, and that the existing relation has been mutually beneficial. Southern slavery has elevated the African to a degree of civilisation which the black race has never attained in any other age or country. "We see it now in its true light, and regard it as the most safe and stable basis for free institutions in the world." Had the slave-trade never been closed, the equilibrium between the North and the South would not have been destroyed. The North has had the Old World from which to draw her supply of labour, and hence the rapid settlement of the north-west. Since 1808, the South has supplied her own labour, and has necessarily made slower progress in settling up the south-west. If the trade were open now, I am persuaded that the South would not consent to close it; and this is perhaps the best answer to the argument derived from the mere sentiment that is arrayed against the proposition. It is apprehended that the opening of this trade will lessen the value of slaves, and ultimately destroy the institution. It is a sufficient answer to point to the fact, that unrestricted immigration has not diminished the value of labour in the north-western section of the confederacy. The cry there is, want of labour, notwithstanding capital has the pauperism of the Old World to press into its grinding service. If we cannot supply the demand for slave-labour, then we must expect to be supplied with a species of labour we do not want, and which is, from the very nature of things, antagonistic to our institutions. In all slaveholding states, true policy dictates that the superior race should direct, and the inferior perform all menial service. Competition between the white and black man for this service may not disturb northern sensibility, but it does not exactly suit our latitude. Irrespective, however, of interest, the act of congress declaring the slave-trade piracy, is a brand upon us which I think it important to remove. If the trade be piracy, the slave must be plunder; and no ingenuity can avoid the logical necessity of such conclusion. My hopes and fortunes are indissolubly associated with this form of society. I feel that I would be wanting in duty if I did not urge you to withdraw your assent to an act which is itself a direct condemnation of our institutions. But we have interests to enforce a course of self-respect. I believe, as I have already stated, that more slaves are necessary to a continuance of our monopoly in plantation products. I believe that they are necessary to the full development of our whole round of agricultural and mechanical resources; that they are necessary to the restoration of the South to an equality of power in the general government, perhaps to the very integrity of slave society, disturbed as it has been by causes which have induced an undue proportion of the ruling race. To us have been committed the fortunes of this peculiar form of society resulting from the union of unequal races. It has vindicated its claim to the approbation of an enlightened humanity. It has civilised and Christianised the African. It has exalted the white race itself to higher hopes and purposes, and it is perhaps of the most sacred obligation that we should give it the means of expansion, and that we should press it forward to a perpetuity of progress.'

In making the foregoing propositions to revive the foreign slave-trade, the more eager spirits of the South do not appear to have sufficiently considered the political difficulties which were presented to a measure of that kind. The North, little as it is to be respected for its general lethargy, would not tolerate so gross an outrage, and it is almost unnecessary to say, that the bare attempt to legalise the importation of slaves, would produce a rupture with England and other European powers, which might end in a speedy solution of the whole question of slavery and colour. The federal authorities hastened to repudiate the sentiments of the extreme southern party. Shortly after the meeting of congress, a resolution was brought into the House of Representatives, December 15, 1856, repelling the notion of opening the slave-trade, and it was carried by a majority of 152 to 57. Immediately afterwards, a resolution was introduced, declaring it to be inexpedient, unwise, and contrary to the settled policy of the United States, to repeal the laws against the slave-trade; and this expression of feeling was carried by a majority of 183 to 8. To think it was necessary at this time of day, for the representatives of a great nation to make these avowals! The motive for doing so, however, is alleged to have been less a regard for the outraged opinion of Christendom, than a desire to discountenance a project for lowering the value of slave-property, which would be an inevitable consequence of large importations of blacks from the coast of Africa. Whatever truth may be in this supposition, surely all except a few indiscreet persons must have felt that southern demonstrations had gone a little too fast—and too far.

SLAVERY AT THE REVOLUTION—ACQUISITION OF LOUISIANA.

IN the dashing times which produced the Declaration of Independence, and opened up the most glowing anticipations of a political millennium, in which we were to 'hold these truths as self-evident, that all men are created equal—that they are endowed by their Creator with certain inalienable rights—that among these are life, LIBERTY, and the pursuit of happiness' —we say, in the midst of these announcements of a brighter day for hitherto down-trodden human nature, and of what was actually done towards founding a great republic, who could have foreseen that in eighty years the result would be a state of things in which a sixth part of the population would be slaves—human beings of every variety of complexion and diversity of intelligence, placed, from no fault of their own, on a level with the brute creation; and further, that this sorrowful and abject condition would come to be extended, perpetuated, vindicated as an essential element in civil society! The world, as it appears to us, has hardly awakened to a consciousness of this historical anomaly; and this is not surprising, for the Americans themselves are as yet only beginning to see the awkwardness of the dilemma into which they have allowed themselves to be drifted.

It was from no qualm of conscience on the part of the committee appointed to draw up the Declaration—Jefferson, Adams, Livingston, Sherman, and Franklin—that the passages relative to slavery were struck out from the celebrated document. 'He [the king of

Great Britain] has waged cruel war against human nature itself, violating its most sacred rights of life and liberty in the persons of a distant people, who never offended him, captivating and carrying them into slavery in another hemisphere, or to incur a miserable death in their transportation thither. This piratical warfare, the opprobrium of infidel powers, is the warfare of the Christian king of Great Britain. Determined to keep open market where men should be bought and sold, he has prostituted his negative for suppressing every legislative attempt to prohibit or to restrain this execrable commerce.' * &c. It was quite as well that these ungentle accusations should have been withdrawn, in consideration, as is said, for the feelings of southern members of the infant confederacy; that so there might remain no historical doubt of the fact, that Union was secured only by conciliating the more intractable order of slaveholders. Whatever, therefore, may be our surprise at the present anomalous complication of American liberty and slavery, the marvel would seem to be lessened by the explanation, that from the very commencement, on that memorable 4th of July 1776, when the Declaration of Independence was signed in the city-hall, Philadelphia, there never has been a condition of universal freedom. The Declaration, doubtless, propounded the doctrine of human equality; but this document never seems to have had the validity of law. At all events, as regards the principle of slavery, the lofty preamble of the Declaration about 'inalienable rights' has proved to be only a respectable piece of

---

* The first draught of the Declaration of Independence, embracing these erased passages, is shewn in the rooms of the American Philosophical Society in Philadelphia, an institution founded by Franklin. It was the greatest archæological curiosity (if such a term be allowable) which the present writer saw in the United States.

Bunkum—words which serve their purpose, and signify nothing.

At the opening of the revolutionary war, there were slaves in all the revolted colonies; even in Massachusetts, the land of the 'Pilgrim Fathers,' there were slaves, and sales of slaves too; though it is proper to add, that Massachusetts was the first to set the example of passing an act for general emancipation.

England, of course, must be charged with the crime of having introduced, in the first instance, the Africans as an article of merchandise into the plantations, against the repeatedly expressed wishes of the settlers, and of having fostered slavery till it took root as a social usage. Lawyers might now speculate on the question—whether, at the period of the revolutionary troubles, slaves could be legally held in the colonies? A short time previously, it had been decided by courts of justice, that a slave landing in England became free; and as the common law was extended over all parts of the realm, it is demonstrable that the maintenance of slavery in distant dependencies was, to say the least of it, open to challenge. The question was not, however, tried; and, as is well known, a vigorous English slave-trade was carried on for many years afterwards with the West Indies and other possessions—much to the profit of Liverpool and Bristol, and apparently to the satisfaction or indifference of all, except the few individuals who deigned to feel an interest in the unhappy objects of ruthless deportation—which individuals, as is usual in such cases, were set down as visionaries, crack-brained enthusiasts, who had no proper regard for national greatness. When the House of Commons was at length induced, in 1792, to pass a bill for the suppression of the slave-trade, it was rejected by the House of Lords, on the ground of its damaging effects upon great commercial and colonial interests. As the famous abolition act did not pass till 1807, and the trade did not absolutely cease till the 1st of January 1808—as, in fact, slaves were held in the colonies until our own times—and, what is still more to the point, as our continued national prosperity depends in no small degree on the purchase and manufacture of slave-grown cotton—the English have not much reason to be boastful on the subject.

For several years after the termination of the revolutionary war—1784 to 1789—the Americans had no proper federal constitution, and public matters were regulated during this interregnum by what was called the Continental Congress, sitting in Philadelphia or New York. To have anything like a correct notion of the American slave question, we need to look back to the operations of this august body. One of the subjects that fell under its discussion, was the management of certain western territories which several states relinquished for the benefit of the general commonwealth, in consideration that congress should liquidate debts and obligations incurred by these states during the war. The cessions were made on these terms; and congress henceforth exercised a direct sovereignty over large tracts of country, from which new states could be excavated. Plans for the government of the Western Territory occupied considerable attention; Mr Jefferson apparently taking a lead in the business, and producing schemes by which slavery was never to be intruded into this vast region. A proposal of this nature was lost on coming to a vote; but at length, in 1787, in the last continental congress, was passed an 'Ordinance for the Government of the Territory of the United States, North-west of the Ohio,' which embraced this provision: 'There shall be neither slavery nor involuntary servitude in the said territory, otherwise than in punishment of crimes, whereof the parties shall be duly convicted.' The enactment of this law, which will afterwards come frequently under notice, would seem to settle the point, that congress is entitled, among other regulations, to enjoin that slavery shall or shall not be a constituent element in the Territories under its special jurisdiction; yet no constitutional question has produced such angry discussion.

The circumstance of Jefferson not being able to carry his larger measure, which comprehended territories south of those just mentioned, shews that the leading men of the time were cramped in their benevolent efforts to extend the sphere of freedom. They were thoroughly aware that slavery in any form, or wherever situated, was a bad thing; and on suitable occasions, they spoke plainly out on the subject. Not disguising the fact from themselves or from others, they nevertheless thought proper to temporise. Believing that any attempt at emancipation through federal agency would probably alienate slaveholders, and so jeopardise the consolidation of the States, they were inclined to leave the subject to the action of public opinion, of which there were hopeful symptoms. As early as 1775, the representatives of a district in Georgia passed a resolution, declaring their disapprobation and abhorrence of the unnatural practice of slavery in America—'a practice,' they say, 'founded on injustice and cruelty, and highly dangerous to our liberties, as well as lives; debasing part of our fellow-creatures below men, and corrupting the virtue and morals of the rest; and as laying the basis of that liberty we contend for on a wrong foundation.' Other anti-slavery sentiments shine out during the ensuing ten years. Massachusetts, as has been said, took the lead in emancipation; other New-England States, and also Pennsylvania, denounce slavery, provide for securing freedom to all born after a certain day, and prohibit the import of any more slaves. Virginia likewise prohibits importation, and removes legal restrictions on emancipation. From North Carolina, New York, and New Jersey, are issued edicts against the further import of slaves. In short, it appears as if slavery was everywhere about to be given up, and done with. Some expectations of this kind, along with an anxiety to conciliate doubtful friends, afford the only excuse for the perpetuation of slavery under the constitution. With a distinct consciousness of its injustice, its dangers, slavery was recognised under ambiguous terms—singular anomaly!—in the great charter of republican freedom. It was competent to repudiate it; it was advisable to maintain a discreet silence respecting it. Neither was done. Here lies the first great blunder of American statesmanship, never to be rectified. The constitution was framed in 1787, and was in general operation in 1789.

This constitution, which still gives cohesion to the States under a federal government, is an instrument divided into articles, each subdivided into clauses. The passages referring to slavery are as follows: In the second clause of the first article there is a provision for representation and taxation—'Representatives and direct taxes shall be apportioned among the several states which may be included within this Union, according to their respective numbers, which shall be determined by adding to the whole number of free persons, including those bound to servitude for a term of years, and excluding Indians not taxed, three-fifths of all other persons.' By 'all other persons' is signified slaves. Accordingly, in whatever state slavery exists, there is till this day a statutory method of making up an artificial constituency: in other words, the number is swelled by counting slaves; but as the slaves have no vote, it happens that a limited constituency of free white persons possess a political power equal to that of a constituency altogether free. That so acute a people as the Americans should have accepted this as a fair thing in representation, and still submit to it, almost passes belief. To proceed, however. The next reference to slavery in the constitution is contained in another clause of the first article—'The migration or importation of such persons as any of the states now existing shall think proper to admit, shall not be prohibited by the congress prior to the year 1808; but a tax or duty may be imposed, not exceeding ten dollars on each person.' By one of the clauses of the fourth article, it is ordained that 'No person held to service or labour in one state under the laws thereof, escaping into another, shall in consequence of any law or regulation therein be discharged from such service or labour, but shall be delivered up on claim of the party to whom such labour may be due.'

Other clauses have a remote bearing on slavery. It is ordained, that 'congress shall have power to suppress insurrections,' and quell 'domestic violence;' consequently, a rebellion of slaves may be suppressed with the whole force that the federal government can bring against it. According to another clause, 'congress shall have power to dispose of, and make all needful rules and regulations respecting the territory or other property belonging to the United States.' How this privilege has been tortured to infer the right of granting permission to extend slavery over new territories, will soon appear.

The use of such ambiguous phraseology in the constitution, as 'persons held to labour,' leads one to infer that the fathers of the constitution were ashamed of the thing indicated. In the face of mankind, and fresh from a successful struggle for liberty, they do not appear to have had the courage to employ a candid phraseology. Be this as it may, the constitution had taken its ground in maintaining the rights of slaveholders. They could hold persons to service, pursue and secure them if they fled; and at least until 1808, they could migrate with them to new possessions, and receive fresh supplies by importation.

Possibly, the national conscience felt no alarm in adopting these legal institutes. All were jubilant over late successes. A mighty power three thousand miles off had been humbled; 'glory,' as Emerson says, had been 'bought cheap.' The new republic could afford to lecture England—which, we are thankful, has always been able to stand a good deal of sound scolding—on the doctrine of inherent human rights. In the address of the first congress under the constitution, to the people of Great Britain, what grandeur in the passages about liberty, oppression, slavery, and chains. ' When a nation, led to greatness by the hand of liberty, and possessed of all the glory that heroism, munificence, and humanity can bestow, descends to the ungrateful task of forging chains for her friends and children, and instead of giving support to freedom, turns advocate for slavery and oppression, there is reason to believe that she has ceased to be virtuous, or has been extremely negligent in the appointment of her rulers.' With such remonstrances against wrong-doing, which seem as if addressed to the living generation of Americans, who could suppose that this same congress required to be reminded that a section of the population was still deprived of its rights? As president of the Abolition Society of Philadelphia, Franklin signed a memorial to the first congress, praying that the blessings of liberty may be rightfully administered, ' without distinction of colour,' and that congress would be pleased to countenance the restoration to liberty of those unhappy men, who alone in a land of freedom are degraded into perpetual bondage.' We all admire the philanthropy breathed in these words; but are unpleasantly reminded that Franklin, with his compatriots, would perhaps have acted more wisely in not constitutionally sanctioning a thing which required afterwards to be spoken of in terms of reprobation.

Let us, however, not bear too hard on the first congress, which in 1789 set a worthy example for future legislation. If the constitution had given congress no power to meddle with slavery in any of the states, it had at least enabled it to regulate the affairs of the territories, from which, both by law and precedent, slavery could be peremptorily excluded. This congress accordingly 'recognised and affirmed the doctrine, embodied by Jefferson in the ordinance of 1787, which for ever excluded slavery from the territory that now embraces Ohio, Indiana, and Illinois [also Iowa and Wisconsin]; and in 1800, the same doctrine was approved by John Adams in the Territorial Act for Indiana.' *

Kept as yet within bounds, and no means being immediately adopted to push slavery beyond certain old limits, the number of 'persons held to labour' in the United States, in 1790, was only 697,897; and as their average market-value was then comparatively small, there could have been no insurmountable difficulty in providing means for their liberation on equitable terms. But no effort of this kind required to be made. The progress of local emancipation which was clearing slavery from the northern, would soon

---

* *America Free, or America Slave—Address to the Citizens of Westchester.* By John Jay, Esq.

remove it from the middle states; and all that the legislators of the day were called on to do was to adopt such measures as would prevent slavery from extending and intrenching itself permanently in the south. Neglectful on this point, all was lost.

Engaged in the task of establishing a great nation— building cities, reclaiming wildernesses, opening up channels of internal communication, extending commerce, planting churches, schools, printing-presses, and other engines of civilisation; successful in almost all arts, and flourishing beyond the hopes of the wildest imagination—the Americans never seem to have attained a clear consciousness that there was any lurking possibility of social dislocation in consequence of slavery being tolerated within their political system. Not that there has not always been a party who augured danger from this quarter; but in the main, things have been left to take their course; or more correctly, the nation has, with singular indifference, seen a series of events successively and more and more hopelessly interweave slavery with the constitution.

It was, we believe, a crotchet of Washington that the federal capital of the United States should be a city removed from popular influences—as if there was any imaginable Olympus from which the pleasant constitutional practice of *Lobbying* could by any stratagem be excluded. New York would not do. Philadelphia—more the pity—would not do. There must be a metropolis standing alone in virtuous solitude, somewhere about the centre of the Union. Accordingly, a site was pitched upon, on the banks of the Potomac, the contiguous states of Virginia and Maryland severally resigning a patch of a few miles square for the purpose, henceforth called the District of Columbia. When Washington here planned and built the city which bears his name, he could not have had any great horror of slavery, although he would much rather there had been no such thing in the world. Virginia and Maryland were then, as now, slave states. Slavery accordingly remained in the District of Columbia, as if indigenous in the soil; and from this time the supreme authorities of the United States became the civic magistracy of a kind of miniature independent state, in which slavery was a recognised institution. It could be shewn that this plantation of a political metropolis in the bosom of slavery did much disservice to the cause of freedom—the sight of slaves, slave-depôts, slave-sales, and the looseness of morals usual in communities affected by slavery, producing no good effect on representatives from the free states. It might be argued that, as Columbia was surrounded by slave states, freedom within this small domain was impracticable. That, however, is not the question. The thing to be deprecated was, making federal authority responsible for an institution which American writers never cease to represent as belonging exclusively to the states in their individual capacity. If any one up till this time imagined that slavery was independent of national administration, his faith, we think, must have received a considerable shock. There were remonstrances, but they sunk and disappeared under a general acquiescence.

We are now referring to the close of the last and beginning of the present century, and shortly afterwards came an event far more serious than the organisation of the capital of the Union. This was a vast accession of new territory on the south and west. Left to themselves, with a wide continent invitingly open for acquisition, the Anglo-Americans only seemed to fulfil an obvious destiny in carrying their flag beyond the limits of the colonies which had been reft from the British crown. A favourable opportunity for making a large acquisition occurred in 1803, when the French under Bonaparte offered to sell the province of Louisiana, which embraced the whole of the west bank of the Mississippi. A little better management on the part of England would perhaps have saved the French the trouble of bargaining away this valuable foreign possession, which they could no longer keep; but as Louisiana was not so secured, it fell naturally, and we must say justifiably, into the hands of the Americans. The purchase, which was made for the sum of fifteen millions of dollars, excited the first of that series of struggles in congress between North and South, which has lasted till our own times. The country acquired, was already settled in its lower part with French slaveholders engaged in the culture of sugar and cotton, and covered an area of about 900,000 square miles—a space larger than all the old thirteen states put together, and including the territories of Missouri, Kansas, and Nebraska, which have latterly engaged so much angry disputation, and caused no little bloodshed.

On the one hand, it was scarcely in human nature to resist the easy acquisition of so splendid a domain; on the other, there were not unreasonable fears among northern politicians that the addition would in some way imperil the security of the Union. Prognostications of disaster, remonstrances, legal doubts, availed not against the controlling desire for national greatness. It mattered not that Washington, in his farewell address to the people of the United States, had uttered the solemn warning—'Let there be no change from usurpation.' It mattered not that Jefferson, at the time president, shewed argumentatively that 'the constitution has made no provision for our holding foreign territory, still less for our incorporating foreign nations into our Union,' and intimated that the acquisition of Louisiana 'would make the constitution blank paper by construction.' Against his better judgment, Jefferson acquiesced in the opinions of those who differed from him, and passed the bill which incorporated Louisiana with the Union. No provision was made for excluding slavery from the ceded territory: the inhabitants, on the contrary, were insured the enjoyment of all their existing property, rights, and privileges; and as the holding of slaves was one of these immunities, it continued, as a matter of course, to be incorporated with the public policy.

The passage of the Louisiana Bill has been justly referred to as the turning-point in the history of the United States. It at once reduced the northern and free communities to an inferior political position, and gave an immense preponderance to the slaveholding interests of the south. In accounting for so extraordinary a change in affairs, the future historian will probably point to other reasons besides the vulgar outcry for national enlargement. He will doubtless find occasion to lament the decline of public spirit. Whether it be that Providence at certain periods sends great men into the world to accomplish particular purposes; or that such at all times latently exist, and are developed into notice by national convulsions; or, to hazard another alternative, that republics are not favourable to the growth of prominent individuals, the fact is undeniable that the great men who effected the American and French revolutions, and who, be it remarked, were bred up under monarchical rule, left behind them no equals in magnitude of intellect or indomitable force of character. It is true that several persons who figured in the commotions of '76 were still on the stage when the Louisiana Bill came under discussion; but there was now a general collapse in heroism; intrigue took the place of patriotic ardour;

the men of the north, for the sake of material interests, succumbed to a course of treatment, which their more sturdy ancestors would not have endured from an English ministry. Unfortunately, also, a deterioration of manners was visible among slaveholders. The gentlemanly spirit of the old planters was passing away. Virginia was beginning to be 'overrun by time-servers, office-hunters, and political blacklegs.' Power was subsiding into the possession of this disreputable class of personages. Nor, all things considered, could much else be expected. Certain radical mistakes, as had been seen, were committed in the general terms of union. The constitutional recognition of slavery had fixed and given breadth to the institution. The slaveholders had secured a franchise to which nothing corresponded in the North. Of course, such a flagrant piece of injustice could not have been tolerated for any length of time, had the North been true to itself. But this, as we may afterwards have occasion to particularise, it has never been—a large proportion of northern men having on all occasions cast in their lot with the political party represented by the more imperious aristocracy of the South. With such facts before us, can we feel surprise at the passage of the Louisiana Bill, and all subsequent bills of the same nature? Freedom had been delivered up, bound hand and foot, to the interests of slavery, and all that followed was a natural consequence of this fundamental error.

We are justified in these opinions by the remarks of the venerable Josiah Quincy, a survivor of the youthful era of the republic. In his late admirable address on this subject, he says: 'The passage of the Louisiana Admission Bill was effected by arts which slaveholders well know how to select and apply. Sops were given to the congressional watch-dogs of the free states. To some, promises were made, by way of opiates; and those whom they could neither pay nor drug, were publicly treated with insolence and scorn. Threats, duels, and violence were at that day, as now, modes approved by them to deter men from awakening the free states to a sense of danger. From the moment the act was passed, they saw that the free states were shorn of their strength; that they had obtained space to multiply slaves at their will; and Mr Jefferson had confidently told them that, from that moment, the "constitution of the United States was blank paper;" but more correctly, there was no longer any constitution. The slaveholders, from that day, saw they had the free states in their power; that they were masters, and the free states slaves; and have acted accordingly. From the passage of the Louisiana Bill until this day, their policy has been directed to a single object, with almost uninterrupted success. That object was to exclude the free states from any share of power, except in subserviency to their views; and they have undeniably, during all the subsequent period of our history (the administration of John Quincy Adams only excepted) placed in the chair of state either slaveholders or men from the free states, who, for the sake of power, consented to be their tools—"Northern men with Southern principles;" in other words, men who, for the sake of power or pay, were willing to do any work they would set them upon.' *

With the widening scope for slave-labour opened up by the passage of the Louisiana Bill, also the contemporary extension of slavery over portions of the southern states, it will not appear strange that in 1810

* *Address Illustrative of the Nature and Power of the Slave States, and the Duties of the Free States:* delivered at Quincy, Massachusetts, June 5, 1856. Boston: Ticknor and Fields.

(notwithstanding the removal of the institution from several states, and the stoppage of the foreign slave-trade in 1808), the number of slaves in the Union had increased to 1,191,364—a significant commentary on the hallucinations of the patriot founders of the republic.

STARTING with lofty notions of liberty and equality, the United States, as already noticed, have always, and now more than ever, been hampered with an institution at variance with public profession, and which —from a European point of view—is lowering in no small degree to national dignity. Seemingly ashamed of slavery as a too obvious fact, American writers hasten to assure us that it is a mere local usage depending on the municipal law of the states in which it happens to exist, and therefore in no way concerns the federal constitution. We are not going to plunge into a political dispute on this point. It is true that slavery derives its vitality from the laws of individual states, and if these laws were severally abrogated, the institution would be no more; but it is equally certain, that while these laws are in operation, the federal power is bound to give them international efficacy. The constitution imparts authority to slaveholders to pursue and seize their property, 'persons held to service,' anywhere within the boundaries of the Union —even where no slavery exists. Besides this old Fugitive Slave-law, lately strengthened by an act of congress, the constitution prescribes a method of making up a constituency to appoint members to the House of Representatives, by reckoning the ratio of free and bond persons. Doubtless, it is unfortunate that the constitution in any manner, however equivocal, recognised and gave force to the practice of holding slaves, and so took that mean stand in the matter of human equality which embarrasses American jurisprudence; but nothing, we think, is to be gained by shirking the fact, and taking a disingenuous view of the subject.

It has been mentioned that the purchase of Louisiana, in 1803, was a turning-point in the history of the Union. At this time, the institution was disappearing from the more northern Atlantic states; and by the celebrated ordinance of 1787, it was excluded from the large Indiana territory on the north-west, from which have been formed the prosperous free states of Ohio, Indiana, Illinois, Michigan, Wisconsin, and Iowa. It lingered still in New York and New Jersey, but southward from Pennsylvania, and westward as far as the banks of the Mississippi, it was as yet confined to the limits of the 'Old Dominion.' Kentucky was formed from a ceded portion of Virginia, Tennessee from North Carolina, and, in like manner, Alabama and Mississippi from portions of Georgia; but though adding to the number of states, and swelling the slaveholding interests in congress, these re-arrangements did not geographically extend the area of slavery.

The acquisition of the French province of Louisiana opened up a boundless prospect for slavery extension. For a number of years, the newly acquired tract of country remained a territory under federal authority. At length, in 1812, the lower part on the Gulf of Mexico was admitted as the state of Louisiana. The remainder of the purchase, stretching northwards on the west bank of the Mississippi, and embracing the rivers Arkansas and Missouri, was henceforth known as the Missouri Territory, over which settlers gradually spread themselves. In March 1818, a sufficient population being consolidated, petitions from the inhabitants were presented to congress, praying for the admission of Missouri as a state. Now began the first resolute struggle between slavery and freedom. It was the wish of the petitioners to have the state admitted on equal terms with the state of Louisiana, in which the inhabitants were guaranteed all the privileges, that of holding slaves among others, which they had enjoyed under the French rule. This was firmly opposed. A degree of alarm concerning the spread of slavery had taken possession of legislators from the free states; and it was felt that now or never was the opportunity for checking its wonderful and unexpected growth in the far west. It must be allowed, that members of congress had been rather late in making this notable discovery—the whole nation, indeed, had been strangely negligent on the subject. If there was a general desire to admit no more states with slavery, the proper precaution would have consisted in enacting a law, like that of the ordinance of 1787, for ever excluding the institution from the territories out of which such states could possibly be formed. The defects of the federal constitution seemed to necessitate such a legislative measure.

It has been graphically said, that when a number of adventurers, British subjects, land on a newly discovered territory, and take possession in the name of the Queen, the common law of England is *ipso facto* established; and from that moment every member of the infant community, no matter what be his breed or colour, enjoys all the privileges, and comes under the usual obligations of free-born Englishmen. In such manner does the British constitution act, and there is a decision and simplicity about it which cannot but command respect. The constitution of the United States is less comprehensive and peremptory. Plant it where you will, it settles no determinate social system. It proclaims freedom, but admits of slavery. All men are free, but freemen may hold slaves—' chattels human'—who though men *de facto*, are seemingly not men *de jure*. The British flag, God knows, has in its day sheltered much insolence, injustice, cruelty. Under it, eighty years ago, an audacious attempt—since regretted and atoned for—was made to rob English colonists of their inherent rights, and what the end of that was, we all know. Things are somewhat altered since Grenville passed the Stamp Act, or since good old Dr Johnson wrote *Taxation no Tyranny*. When we see the Union Jack floating from a vessel in the Atlantic, we feel a sound assurance that there is not the vestige of a slave on board. A sight of the American flag does not convey the same confidence; seen south from the capes of Virginia, two to one it is covering a cargo of slaves on the way to the market for 'chattels human' at New Orleans; for though the foreign slave-trade terminated in 1808, the coasting slave-trade did not, and is till this day in full operation. If this be thought a hard view of practices prevailing under the federal constitution, we cannot help it. The constitution is not that of a distinct nation, but simply the terms of compact by which a number of sovereignties—at present thirty-one—agree to hold together for the sake of mutual convenience and purposes common to the whole. Some of these sovereignties exclude slavery, some maintain it. The federal constitution, consequently, operates with considerable reserve on this delicate subject. It is anything you like to make of it. When extended over new territories, unless congress interpose an order to the contrary, the choice of domestic institutions is nominally left to the parties concerned. If, when the time comes, they choose to inaugurate slavery, good and well; it is all the same to the constitution. This is called 'freedom.' So much for theory. Let us now see how the thing practically works.

When a new tract of country is acquired by the United States, it passes into the possession and under the control of the federal authorities, who hold it for the general behoof. If it be resolved to lay it out for a new state, it is first created a 'territory.' As such, it is the subject of an act of congress, from which body it receives an interim constitution, prescribing its boundaries, divisions, executive authorities, laws, judicial and political system. With a governor appointed by the president, it remains under federal tutelage, till on petition of its inhabitants it is admitted into the sisterhood of states. All this seems reasonable, and, in its general features, the practice affords a fine instance of that self-creative political organisation for which the Americans are celebrated. Analysing the acts of congress and presidents, we observe something less favourable. The federal constitution is silent about race or colour; but in interpreting it, American lawgivers arrive at the conclusion, that the United States are the property of whites, and that persons with a tinge of dark colour in their countenance, though born free, are not citizens. A short time ago, this view of citizenship was enforced by a high federal officer, one of the secretaries of state, who refused passports to some coloured free persons, on the ground that they 'were not citizens within the meaning of the constitution.' This may be a right or a wrong interpretation of the fundamental charter of the Union: it is, at all events, acted on without apparently exciting public challenge. Accordingly, in passing an act to organise a territory—as, for example, that of 1854, constituting the territories of Nebraska and Kansas—there is the following regulation in regard to voters: 'Every free white male inhabitant, twenty-one years old, an actual resident in the territory at the time of the passage of this act, and with the qualifications after described, may vote,' &c. Thus, at the very outset, a disqualification is imposed on free coloured persons, without the slightest regard to their means or their ability; and from this to 'holding persons to service,' is an easy transition. Such, however, are the prejudices against colour in the United States, that the most ardent lovers of freedom in Kansas, while suffering from pro-slavery aggression, never proposed to give the franchise to any but whites.

The federal constitution being indifferent to the spread or limitation of slavery, the will of congress and president for the time being is a kind of supplemental constitution, whence the internal policy of a new territory is moulded. Much usually depends on the political leanings of the president, who, being irremovable for four years, and armed with an enormous power of appointment to office, may be said to exercise a control more resembling that of a despot than a constitutional sovereign. The presidents of past times have, for the most part, had strong pro-slavery convictions, and thrown the balance of authority in that direction. Still affecting to allow fair-play in the scramble between slavery and anti-slavery principles in the inchoate states, they would rather seem to have aided in imparting to them pro-slavery constitutions. Mr Pierce, the late president, thought that if things are left to take their course in a territory, slavery, from its intrinsic qualities, will outstrip freedom. In his late message to congress, he says: 'It is the fact that in all the unsettled regions of the United States, if emigration be left free to act in this respect for itself, without legal prohibitions on either side, slave labour will spontaneously go everywhere in preference to free labour. Is it the fact that the peculiar domestic institutions of the southern states possess relatively so much of vigour, that wheresoever an avenue is freely open to all the world, they will penetrate, to the exclusion of those of the northern states?' Leaving the North to answer Mr Pierce's question, it is enough for us to know that the pretended freedom communicated by congress and the constitution, produces an unseemly fracas in territorial organisation; so that ever and anon a battle is raging somewhere in the south or west.

The act being passed which throws open the territory for settlement, a rush ensues from all points in the Union. Lawyers, schoolmasters, printers, and preachers from Massachusetts; farmers from Vermont and New Hampshire; mechanics and pedlers from Connecticut; storekeepers from Cincinnati, Philadelphia, and New York; planters with bands of 'servants' from Alabama and Kentucky; and loafers, rowdies, and ragamuffins from everywhere, are hastening on by steam-boat, railway, wagon, horseback, wheel-barrow, and on foot to the land of promise—struggling, pushing, driving, drinking, swearing, cheating, and it may be, fighting. The rule, if there be a rule, is every man for himself. The great thing is, who shall get the earliest clutch at the best localities; and not much ceremony is used in squatting and taking possession. In no time, a capital city is planted, hotels struck up, a state-house inaugurated, newspapers set agoing, and voting for territorial, civic, and judicial officers is in 'full blast.' In one sense, there is something grand in this restless onflow of Anglo-Americans over the domains of unreclaimed nature. We are carried in imagination back to that most ancient of injunctions, 'to go forth to replenish the earth, and subdue it.' To be sure, the thing is done coarsely—very. But it is done somehow; and from the chaos of a first settlement, spring in due time order and civilisation. What we have occasion to deplore is, the totally unnecessary and undesirable scramble for slavery or freedom in the new settlements. We need hardly say that, according to all accounts, the slaveholding interests take care to assume such a dictatorial attitude in these freshly opened lands, that under favour of the federal executive, they are able to overawe opposition, and to prefer claims to congress for a pro-slavery constitution, which cannot well be withstood. That congress should all the while complacently stand aside, on the presumption that a free choice is to be made, and at last legislate on this understanding, seems only to be a method of wilfully extending slavery to the further limits of the Union. Of course, should congress attempt to legislate prospectively in favour of freedom, it will have imputed to it that it is unconstitutionally taking a side—doing what it has no business to do; acting as umpire between free and slave states. There are grounds, however, for believing that congress possesses authority to exclude slavery from the territories. Jefferson's ordinance of 1787, excluding it from the north-west territory, was an enactment of the last continental congress, which has been repeatedly recognised and sanctioned by the federal congress. It is evident, therefore, that until a new and more comprehensive federal constitution is adopted—if ever that will be—the proper course of policy, if it be at all practicable amidst party contentions, is for congress to pass a general enactment, for ever excluding slavery from all the territories of the United States. Mr Buchanan, we believe, maintains the doctrine, that the constitution limits the power of congress in this respect; while, on the contrary, his late opponent, Colonel Fremont, holds to the opinion that congress is constitutionally entitled 'to prohibit in the territories those twin-relics of barbarism—polygamy and slavery.' Moderate men of all parties, we should think, would wish to see congress resolutely embrace this latter opinion; but in order to do so with any chance of success, northern men would require to abandon that singularly temporising policy—that anomalous subserviency to southern interests—for which they have earned an unenviable reputation. It is notorious, that with all the prevalent alarm respecting the increasing power of slaveholders, and all the professions in favour of freedom, the North expresses no desire to do more than seclude slavery within a certain geographical limit. That this has generally been the hapless policy of the free portion of the Union, is conspicuous in the history of the Missouri Compromise and subsequent events.

We now approach this famed Compromise. In February 1819, the petition of the inhabitants of Missouri for the admission of their state, which had been some time under consideration, led to a hot debate in congress. In the House of Representatives, Mr Tallmadge of New York moved the following amendment on the proposed constitution: 'And provided that the introduction of slavery, or involuntary servitude, be prohibited, except for the punishment of crimes, whereof the party has been duly convicted, and that all children born within the said state, after the admission thereof into the Union, shall be declared free at the age of twenty-five years.' To this restriction, southern members objected, for the reason that congress had no right to impose such offensive terms. Missouri was entitled, like every other state, to choose its own institutions, so far as slavery was concerned. Threats were thrown out, that if the restriction were carried, the South would dissolve its connection with the Union. Tallmadge, who appears to have been a man of dauntless energy, referred to this new outcry: 'If a dissolution of the Union must take place, let it be so. If civil war, which gentlemen so much threaten, must come, I can only say, let it come. My hold on life is probably as frail as that of any man who now hears me; but while that hold lasts, it shall be devoted to the service of my country—to the freedom of man. If blood is necessary to extinguish any fire which I have assisted to kindle, I can assure gentlemen, while I regret the necessity, I shall not forbear to contribute my mite. Sir, the violence to which gentlemen have resorted on this subject will not move my purpose, nor drive me from my place. I have the fortune and the honour to stand here as the representative of freemen, who possess intelligence to know their rights—who have the spirit to maintain them. As their representative, I will proclaim their hatred to slavery in every shape—as their representative, here will I hold my stand, till this floor, with the constitution of my country which supports it, shall sink beneath me—if I am doomed to fall, I shall at least have the painful consolation to believe that I fall as a fragment in the ruins of my country.' Referring to menaces of violence, he continued: 'Has it already come to this: that in the congress of the United States—that in the legislative councils of republican America, the subject of slavery has become a subject of so much feeling—of such delicacy—of such danger, that it cannot be safely discussed! Are we to be told of the dissolution of the Union, of civil war, and of seas of blood? And yet, with such awful threatenings before us, do gentlemen in the same breath insist upon the encouragement of this evil; upon the extension of this monstrous scourge of the human race? An evil so fraught with such dire calamities to us as individuals, and to our nation, and threatening in its progress to overwhelm the civil and religious institutions of the country, with the liberties of the nation, ought at once to be met, and to be controlled. If its power, its influence, and its impending dangers, have already arrived at such a point that it is not safe to discuss it on this floor, and it cannot now pass under consideration as a proper subject for general legislation, what will be the result when it is spread through your widely extended domain? Its present threatening aspect, and the violence of its supporters, so far from inducing me to yield to its progress, prompt me to resist its march. Now is the time. It must now be met, and the extension of the evil must now be prevented, or the occasion is irrecoverably lost, and the evil can never be controlled.'

Next, alluding to the extension of empire over the vast territories of the west, Tallmadge says: 'People this fair domain with the slaves of your planters; extend *slavery*, this bane of man, this abomination of Heaven, over your extended empire, and you prepare its dissolution; you turn its accumulated strength into positive weakness; you cherish a canker in your breast; you put poison in your bosom; you place a vulture preying on your heart—nay, you whet the dagger and place it in the hands of a portion of your population, stimulated to use it by every tie, human and divine. The envious contrast between your happiness and their misery, between your liberty and their slavery, must constantly prompt them to accomplish your destruction. Your enemies will learn the source and the cause of your weakness. As often as external dangers shall threaten, or internal commotions await you, you will then realise that, by your own procurement, you have placed amidst your families, and in the bosom of your country, a population producing at once the greatest cause of individual danger and of national weakness. With this defeat, your government must crumble to pieces, and your people become the scoff of the world.'

Finally, the bill embodying the restriction was lost. The men of the north, we have said, strangely content themselves with seeing slavery fortify and extend itself, provided it keep within a certain limit. The required line of division appears to be that which bounds the cotton-producing lands of the south. Having lost Missouri territory, as a whole, the friends of freedom did not prevent the southern portion of it being organised as a territory, without any restriction as to slavery. This was accordingly done. Arkansas was set off as a distinct territory; and the usual means being employed to give it pro-slavery tendencies, it became ultimately (1836) a slave state.

The struggle about Missouri was renewed in December 1819 and January 1820. As there seemed no possibility of reconciling both branches of congress to a plan of restriction within Missouri, the idea of a compromise was suggested. It was proposed by Mr Thomas of Illinois to admit Missouri as a slave state; but, as a compensation, to exclude it prospectively from all the remainder of the old Louisianan territory, north of a certain latitude. His provision was—
'And be it further enacted, That in all that territory ceded by France to the United States under the name of Louisiana which lies north of thirty-six degrees thirty minutes, north latitude, excepting only such part thereof as is included within the limits of the state contemplated by this act, slavery and involuntary servitude, otherwise than in the punishment of crime whereof the party shall have been duly convicted, shall be, and is hereby for ever prohibited.' This compromise, after various divisions in both houses, was adopted. Missouri was enabled to enter the Union as a slave state. There was yet, however, another struggle connected with this troublesome matter. When the Missourians, in November 1820, submitted their state

constitution to the approval of congress, it was found to contain some objectionable clauses, preventing the settlement of free men of colour in the state. As several northern states acknowledge free coloured men to be citizens, though the federal constitution, as usually interpreted, is much more exclusive, the objectionable clauses met with a warm opposition. At this juncture, a new character comes on the stage. Throughout the whole Missouri affair, Henry Clay, a statesman of no mean eminence, had given the aid of his counsels. If every man has his mission, Clay's seems to have been that of inventing compromises. He was an orator, a schemer—one of those mighty geniuses who have always a plan in their pocket to tide over difficulties, and who, in securing present peace, do not mind sowing the seeds of future discord. Clay's plan of engineering a difficulty was sublimely simple. It consisted in compounding for so much evil by so much good. If a certain quantity of slavery was put in one scale, the same quantity of freedom, *or what looked like freedom*, was put in the other; so the balance was adjusted, and all parties satisfied. He is understood to have been the real concocter of the Missouri Compromise; and now, at this fresh and unexpected collision, he interposed with a scheme of settlement. It consisted in exacting a pledge from the Missouri legislature, that no advantage should be taken of its constitution, and it should pass no act 'to exclude any of the citizens of either of the states' from the enjoyment of the privileges they enjoy under the constitution of the United States. This qualifying provision was accepted. The only question is—who are 'citizens within the meaning of the constitution?' So ended the contests about Missouri, which was received into the Union as a full-blown slave state—a circumstance ever to be regretted, for, independently of other considerations, the state, as will be seen on looking at a map, projects considerably northward into free territory, and so stops the way to free migration westward.

SYMPATHISING with the Americans in their unfortunate inheritance of slavery, and making every allowance for the constitutional difficulties which are presumed to surround any plan for its eradication, we must regret the manner in which this portentous evil has not only been suffered but actually stimulated to grow in dimensions. At no period since the foundation of the Union, has the number of slaves diminished; on the contrary, it has regularly increased; and at the period at which our narrative has arrived, 1820, it amounted to 1,538,064.

From the time the Missouri Compromise came under agitation, there was a succession of measures, all calculated to extend the sphere of compulsory servitude. The first of these was the annexation of Florida, which did not excite any particular hostility. The peninsula of Florida—swampy, rich in alluvial marshes and savannahs, and eminently suitable for the production of rice and the sugar-cane—possesses a history abounding in picturesque incident. Discovered and settled by the Spaniards; captured by the English; then rendered back to the Spaniards; it ultimately, during the early years of the present century, became an object of desire to the United States—to which, by contiguity, it formed so convenient an appendage, that its fate from the outset could easily have been foretold.

The Americans, as their best friends allow, have never, on suitable occasions, been at a loss to make out a good case of injury, requiring smart reparation.

The Floridans were a bad set. They had preyed like freebooters on American commerce, and the sufferers were denied all redress from Spain; they had excited the Indians to molest the frontiers of the states; and, worst of all, they had given refuge to runaway slaves from Georgia and Louisiana. Such proceedings were intolerable. Pacific overtures having failed, the United States government despatched a military force to overrun Florida. Negotiations followed, in which the Americans advanced a claim to Texas, as having been a portion of the old French province of Louisiana, which the Spaniards ought long since to have relinquished. Spain was thankful to buy off this strange demand, and otherwise adjust the claims against it, by ceding Florida; the United States at the same time undertaking to indemnify American citizens for their losses. In virtue of a treaty to this effect, Florida was taken possession of by General Jackson in the summer of 1821. As a territory of the Union, this hapless peninsula endured for some time the horrors of a war levied against the Seminole Indians, with a view to recover fugitive slaves and their descendants. The narrative of this ruthless war of races, aggravated by the use of blood-hounds to trace the Indians and negroes through the brakes and swamps, involves instances of more fearful suffering and daring heroism than perhaps any history of modern times. Finally, the Indians being subdued and removed in a body, and the real or alleged fugitives secured, Florida settled down into the ordinary condition of a state, with slavery as a legalised institution.

The claim on Texas on the above occasion, shewed pretty conclusively that there were parties in the United States who cast a longing eye in that direction. The practice of acquiring new countries and adding them to the Union, began with Louisiana and Florida, and with these precedents, might be carried to any extent. The desire for these territorial acquisitions, though partly owing to the restless character of the Americans, as well as to certain necessities in their position, arose in no small degree from causes connected with slavery. Not to speak of the exhaustion of lands by slave-labour, and the corresponding obligation to seek for fresh scenes of operation, there is an incessant natural increase in the slave population, which leaves to planters no choice between being eaten up by servants, sending them adrift through the agency of the slave-trader, or causing their sons to remove with detachments to new lands. On this account alone, there is positively no limit to the extension of slavery. Unless the surplus be carried off by emancipation—and to that the law in several states presents serious obstacles—there is no restricting it in amount or keeping it within a definite locality. Then, we have the commercial principle giving active impulse to the institution. Slave breeders and traders rejoice in the prospect of new settlements and new purchasers; and if the matter rested with them, they would be glad to see the Union ingulf country after country, till at length there was nothing more to incorporate. To this wild demand for territorial enlargement, the central government, for obvious reasons, can give no external concurrence in the first instance; but that is of little consequence.

The condition of affairs in America is at all times favourable to the commission of daring exploits by private adventurers, whose acts can be repudiated or sanctioned as circumstances shall determine. In no country in Europe could be found groups of individuals at all to compare with these adventurers, of the true filibuster type. They are the refuse of the world —penniless, reckless, confident, and unscrupulous.

Refugee Poles, Italians, and Frenchmen; exiles from the British Islands, bankrupt in character and fortune; Portuguese and Spaniards, with predatory habits acquired in the slave-trade or in freebooting; immigrant Germans, who, instead of pushing off to inland rural settlements, as is usual with their countrymen, have become frequenters of taverns, and copiously indulge in 'lager beer;' sons of American gentlemen, who, brought up without restraint, and having gone through their fortune, loiter about bar-rooms and gaming-houses, get up dog and cock fighting matches, and at night tormenting the streets as rowdies—all are ready for any sort of mischief. Such are some of the elements of a filibustering expedition, of which, however, the 'white trash' of the south, by whom honest labour is deemed a disgrace, usually form the staple material. Equip, arm, and ship off company after company of this heterogeneous mass—see them land in grotesque costume, their trousers stuffed into dirty boots, their red woollen shirts, their rusty beards, hats of every imaginable shape, belts stuck with bowie-knives and revolvers, and rifles slung over their shoulders—chewing, spitting, swearing—and you have an army of marauders such as, we venture to say, could be nowhere else produced on the face of the earth.

Nature accomplishes great designs by rough agencies. The Old World was not peopled and settled as we now see it, without going through centuries of violence and bloodshed. Greeks, Persians, Romans, Goths, Saxons, Normans, and Sea-kings, all in their turn conquered without justice or mercy. But that was long ago, and one imagines that, under the lights of Christianity and modern civilisation, things should be managed differently. True in one respect, but not in another. Much of the American continent is now going through its ancient and middle ages. Filibusters are the Sea-kings of the nineteenth century. Who is to restrain them, so long as they confine their stealthy attacks to regions under a weak rule, adjoining the southern states, and the annexation of which to the Union flatters the desire for national aggrandisement? If to this we add the ardent demand for new territories over which to disseminate slave-labour, the impulse for acquisition not only becomes irresistible, but, to judge from past events, is almost certain to receive the countenance of the highest federal authorities.

Looking about for means of advancing their interests, slaveholders and slave-traders saw no outlet so available as that westward along the Gulf of Mexico into Texas. This province, of almost matchless fertility, producing cotton equal to the finest in the United States, extended over twelve degrees of latitude, with an area large enough to form eight or nine ordinary sized states; and it was calculated that, if freely opened to planters and their servants, the value of human stock would probably rise fifty per cent. Ever seeking new spots for settlement, parties of emigrants had begun to find homes in Texas as early as 1819. They were chiefly from the north, and, for the sake of material interests, were fain to submit to the petty tyranny which usually accompanies the Spanish rule. Some years elapsed before there appeared any chance of success for a filibustering expedition. As soon as Mexico had shaken off Spain, and declared itself a republic, things seemed ripe for striking a blow. From this time, 1834-5, we hear of migration into Texas on a formidable scale. It is no longer parties of industrious yeomen who come across the frontier, but companies of armed men, under southern leaders of military reputation. Claiming to have territorial rights under grants from Mexican authorities, there arrive in their train, flocks of greedy speculators and jobbers, holders of scrip in real or pretended joint-stock land companies, besides a floating mass of adventurers anxious to secure whatever good might fall in their way—and when we recollect that there was a country as large as France to be won by dint of a little impudence and fighting, and that the first-comers had the best chance, the rush to Texas is no great matter for surprise. The method of appropriation, however, is curious. It resembles nothing so much as that of a lodger who, taking a fancy to his quarters, begins by finding fault with his landlord, and ends with turning him out of doors. Clearly, the Americans had no business in Texas—not any more than the English had in India—and if they went thither, it was their duty as foreigners to remain quiet. But good order and respect for rights are, in such cases, against all rule. How the Texan settlers and their allies picked endless quarrels with the wretched government to which the province nominally belonged—how, under General Sam. Houston, the invading host unfurled the standard of rebellion—the significant lone-star—which like a meteor they carried through the country, as far as the banks of the Rio Grande del Norte—how they overpowered the Mexicans, and in one of their battles captured Santa Anna, whom they set at liberty only on having conceded to them the independence of Texas—are all circumstances well known. In short, in the space of two years, by the desultory movements of a body of unauthorised adventurers, an extensive and valuable province was wrested from Mexico. The brilliance of this exploit is somewhat lessened by the fact, that a large army entered Texas, by order of the United States government, professedly to allay Indian disturbances, but really to hang about as a reserve, to countenance, and, if need be, to support, the filibusters. The object of the invasion was never a matter of doubt. It was to secure independence, and then to seek annexation, with a view to strengthening southern interests, by adding several new slaveholding states to the Union. On the character of this splendid manœuvre, we should prefer allowing an American writer to speak. 'Some crimes by their magnitude,' says Channing, 'have a touch of the sublime; and to this dignity the seizure of Texas by our citizens is entitled. Modern times furnish no example of individual rapine on so grand a scale. It is nothing less than the robbery of a realm. The pirates seize a ship. The colonists and their coadjutors satisfy themselves with nothing short of an empire.' Shrinking from annexation, he adds that this act will be accomplished only at the 'imminent peril' of American 'institutions, union, prosperity, virtue, and peace.' *

In the wilful perpetuation and extension of slavery—its infliction on a country from which it was expelled—lies, perhaps, the chief odium of this great deed of spoliation. Although accustomed to look with contempt on Spain and the transatlantic nations which she has planted, we are obliged in the present instance, as an act of simple justice, to state, that when the Mexicans attained independence, they at the same time loosened the bonds of the slave—decreeing, 'that no person thereafter should be born a slave, or introduced as such into the Mexican states; that slaves then held should receive stipulated wages, and be subject to no punishment but on trial and judgment of the magistrate.' Doubtless, these humane provisions were partly a consequence of the large infusion of mixed

* *Channing's Letter to the Hon. Henry Clay, on the Annexation of Texas.* 1837.

breeds and persons of colour in all ranks of Mexican society; but be this as it may, slavery had been abolished in Texas when it fell into the hands of the Americans. After this occurrence, however, slaves were rapidly introduced, and with avowed slavery institutions, the republic claimed to be admitted into the Union. When annexation was formally proposed, there was a considerable division of opinion as to its expediency. Petitions were presented to congress, and Daniel Webster, among other men of note, offered some wholesome oratorical opposition to the measure, on the ground that the admission of so large a region as Texas would give a most undue preponderance to the South. In one of his speeches, he says: 'I frankly avow my entire unwillingness to do anything which shall extend the slavery of the African race on this continent, or add other slaveholding states to the Union. When I say that I regard slavery in itself a great moral, social, and political evil, I only use language which has been adopted by distinguished men, themselves citizens of slaveholding states. I shall do nothing, therefore, to favour or encourage its further extension. In my opinion, the people of the United States will not consent to bring a new, vastly extensive, and slaveholding country, large enough for half-a-dozen or a dozen states, into the Union. IN MY OPINION, THEY OUGHT NOT TO CONSENT TO IT. Indeed, I am altogether at a loss to conceive what possible benefit any part of this country can expect to derive from such annexation. All benefit to any part is at least doubtful and uncertain—the objections obvious, plain, and strong. On the general question of slavery, a great portion of the community is already strongly excited. The subject has not only attracted attention as a question of politics, but it has struck a far deeper-toned chord—it has arrested the religious feeling of the country; it has taken a strong hold on the consciences of men. He is a rash man, indeed, and little conversant with human nature, and especially has he a very erroneous estimate of the character of the people of this country, who supposes that a feeling of this kind is to be trifled with or despised. It will assuredly cause itself to be respected.' In conclusion, he said: 'I see, therefore, no political necessity for the annexation of Texas to the Union—no advantages to be derived from it, and objections to it of a strong, and, in my judgment, decisive character. I believe it to be for the interest and happiness of the whole Union to remain as it is, without diminution and without addition.'

Expostulation was useless. By the election of Mr Polk as president, November 1844, the people shewed their desire for annexation. When the subject was debated in congress, a resolution to annex was carried, and Texas was accordingly incorporated as a state in 1845, without any restriction as to slavery. It was provided that four new states of convenient size might afterwards be formed out of it; and further, that slavery, at the discretion of the inhabitants, might exist in all the new states, south of 36° 30′ north latitude, commonly known as the Missouri Compromise line.

Out of the annexation of Texas sprung a war, which in its turn produced still greater extensions of the Union. According to Mexican topography, the boundary of Texas on the west was the river Nueces. The Texans, however, insisted that the proper limit was the Rio Grande del Norte; and in 1846, an army of occupation under General Taylor was marched into the disputed region. On this and some other grounds of dispute, a collision with the Mexicans ensued; and for two years subsequently, there raged a war by sea and land with the United States. The result, as might have been expected, was disastrous to the Mexicans, who were no match for the Americans. Under General Scott, the war was prosecuted with consummate skill, and nothing could have been more easy than the conquest of the whole of Mexico, had it been expedient to carry matters that length. By the final terms of adjustment, the United States government paid large sums to Mexico for extensive tracts of country which might have been retained or taken by force. The possessions acquired on this occasion included California, and certain regions in the interior, now composing the territories of New Mexico and Utah—in fact, by these annexations, in conjunction with rights founded on pre-occupation, the dominion of the United States engrossed the entire continent from the Atlantic to the Pacific, and from the British possessions on the north to the shrunken republic of Mexico on the south; and it seemingly became only a question of expediency as to the time when all that remained of Mexico should swell the gigantic proportions of the Union.

To procure a command of money for the purchases from Mexico, a bill of appropriation was laid before congress. Now ensued a long and entangled contest between parties respecting the restriction or non-restriction of slavery in the lands about to be acquired from Mexico; it was, in fact, a resumption of the old dispute, whether congress had the power to determine the institutions of the territories. The debate in the first instance turned on the motion of Mr David Wilmot of Pennsylvania, usually called the Wilmot proviso, which was to the effect of passing the bill, 'provided neither slavery nor involuntary servitude shall ever exist in any part of the territory to be acquired from Mexico.' This and similar restrictive clauses were lost. In the succeeding congress, 1847, a bill was carried to organise the territory of Oregon, according to the provisions in the ordinance of 1787. This latter point, which insured freedom to the territory, was carried with some difficulty. It may here be added, that the territory of Minnesota was organised, 1849, and that of Washington, 1853; both have free institutions. The northern situation of these territories, we presume, rendered them not very available for slavery.

During the passage of the Oregon bill, an attempt was made by the slaveholding interest to extend the line 36° 30′ to the Pacific; but it was defeated. The object of the movement was, in effect, to make a distinct division of the United States into North and South, each with its peculiar institutions. Such a division was felt to be essential to the permanence of slavery; for if, at any subsequent period, free states should be organised on the borders of Texas, they would be a ready refuge for the whole slave population. The defeat of the proposed division, which was a kind of northern triumph, did no more, however, than postpone for a short time the tug of war. Hitherto, while there were plenty of new lands north and south to annex, free and slave states had been added in so equal a proportion, that the numerical balance was kept tolerably even. Now, the unoccupied lands in the north were becoming scarce; many new free states in that direction were hopeless; and if the balance was to be maintained, the North would require to seek for an equipoise south of the line of the Missouri Compromise. The game of pitching new states into the Union was getting serious—the result critical.

Nations, like individuals, usually add more to their cares than their comforts by their acquisitions of property. The United States had from small beginnings become a mighty empire; but while prosperous in its material interests, it was vexed with intestine commotions. It had acquired enormously large possessions in the south; but what was to be done with them? Eager discussions respecting these acquisitions occurred in congress, 1849-50. Zachary Taylor, the new president, having recommended the organisation of California as a state, and New Mexico and Utah as territories, of the Union, there arose a contest on that everlasting subject—the imposition of restrictions as to slavery. Once more, Henry Clay interposes to allay the storm with an ingeniously complicated and specious compromise. To understand the purport of this beautiful piece of legislation, it is necessary to have some notion of the state of affairs since 1834. The invasion of Texas, and its probable results in extending slavery, greatly stimulated the party of Abolitionists, who about this time began to agitate with uncommon zeal—perhaps more zeal than discretion—through the agency of speeches, pamphlets, and petitions. One of the things they especially demanded was the expulsion of slavery from the District of Columbia, where it was a scandal to the official capital of the States. So numerous were the petitions presented to congress on this and analogous subjects, that at length the extraordinary resolution to receive no more was adopted, and for several years the very right of petition was so far suspended. It was during this turbulent decade (1830-40), that a bill was brought in to extend the slave state of Missouri. The prescribed boundaries of this state on the west having excluded a triangular district, which remained free soil in virtue of the ordinance of 1787, the incorporation of it was anxiously desired by the Missourians, for it was exceedingly fertile, and lay on the route to the rich and still unappropriated lands of Kansas.

Strange to say, the bill to incorporate this region —legally insured to freedom—was passed in 1836 without any perceptible opposition. The tract so annexed composes six counties, and has become one of the most populous and wealthy sections of the state, devoted to the growing of hemp, tobacco, and other articles, and cultivated by slaves. This, we are told, 'is the most pro-slavery section of the state, in which was originated, and has been principally sustained, that series of inroads into Kansas, corruptions of her ballot-boxes, and outrages on her people, which have earned for their authors the appellation of *border ruffians.*' *

Not discouraged, the ultra anti-slavery party kept up a constant war of argument and remonstrance through the press. The Texan invasion and its consequences imparted fresh energy to the remonstrants. Petitions for a dissolution of the Union, for amendments in the constitution, for a reform of the representation, were poured into congress, and when discussions arose respecting the admission of California, the contest overshadowed all other questions. Clay, as has been said, now comes on the scene, with his plan of conciliation, which, being embodied in several bills, was cleverly carried through congress in August 1850. This famous 'omnibus' measure, as it was called, was worthy of Clay's genius. The South had complaints against the North, on account of the difficulties thrown in the way of recovering fugitive slaves. The North complained that slavery continued to exist in the District of Columbia. Clay projected some mutual concession on these points; and as the South was the more intractable, adjusted its demands

---

* *History of the Struggle for Slavery Extension or Restriction.* By Horace Greeley. Dix & Edwards, New York, 1856.

by conceding that the inhabitants of the new southern acquisitions should exercise the right of introducing or excluding slavery; further, the original compact with Texas was confirmed, and its western boundary fixed at the Rio Grande del Norte. California was admitted as a state, and New Mexico and Utah as territories, on the basis of 'squatter sovereignty'—a circumstance of no moment, as it proved, to California, which, though already intruded on by some planters and their slaves, made choice of freedom. Slavery was not abolished in Columbia, but the slave-trade and open sales of slaves were prohibited under heavy penalties in the District. Lastly, the Fugitive Slave Bill strengthened those provisions in the federal constitution for recovering runaways, which in many parts of the country had become practically inoperative.

These united measures did not become law without incurring opposition on both sides; but we are concerned to observe, that in all the divisions in the legislature, members from free states voted with the South—the only rational explanation of this being, that the principle of freedom *versus* slavery had not attained force sufficient to overcome party connection or individually selfish considerations. Among the eminent men who on this occasion voted in violation of formerly professed principles, was Daniel Webster—a circumstance of which he was so painfully reminded by his rejection at a convention for proposing candidates for the presidentship, that he languished and died 'a damaged man,' October 1852. Clay, a short time before, made an equally abrupt and unlamented exit.

It is now, we believe, generally admitted by its partisans, that Clay's Fugitive Slave Bill was a grave political blunder; for, besides failing in its professed object, it caused considerable exasperation in the northern states, in some of which it is already as much a dead-letter as were the original obligations on which it was founded. So much for Clay's omnibus measure, which was to insure universal harmony! So much for what a committee of congress in 1854, sagaciously proclaimed as having been 'a final settlement of the controversy, and an end of the agitation.' Well may one say, with how little wisdom is the world governed!

With the incentives to increase, to which we have drawn attention, it will not be thought remarkable that in 1850, the number of slaves in the United States had risen to 3,204,313.

It will be recollected that on the occasion of constituting the state of Missouri, in 1820, there was a compromise among parties to the effect that, in all the territory which had been ceded by France north of 36° 30′, the state of Missouri excepted, slavery should be for ever prohibited; and the act which admitted the state to the Union bore a clause of this kind. Here was a law settling the question so far, one would think. Events proved that this was not so certain. Missouri having edged itself in as a slave state, there the affair rested; and when, in 1836, a slice of fresh free territory was added to this slave state, the compromise clause does not appear to have been agitated. It was reserved for Mr Pierce's first congress to be troubled with the resurrection of a measure which the bulk of the members—and Pierce to boot—had probably begun to hope was past being brought to life. On the 15th of December 1853, a bill was submitted to the senate to organise the territory of Nebraska; and on this occasion the unhappy compromise rises from the dead. Let us look at our maps, and see where lies the region which was to provoke one of the severest party contests that has ever occurred in or out of congress.

Nebraska was the name at first given to a large tract of country, having on the east Missouri, Iowa, and Minnesota, and stretching from 36° 30′ or thereabouts, to the borders of Canada. Its limits on the west were New Mexico, Utah, Oregon, and Washington. The more eastern portion of this vast territory, was fertilised by the rivers Platte, Kaw or Kansas, and other tributaries of the Missouri, and its only occupants were certain tribes of Indians. The rich lands on the borders of the rivers, and beyond them the rolling and flowery prairies, were, however, becoming too attractive to be much longer exempted from the ever-operating law of Anglo-American migration. The federal government had begun to cause regular explorations west of Missouri, about 1838, but on so imperfect a scale, that fresh and much more extensive investigations were ordered in 1842; the commander of the scientific explorers on this occasion being Lieutenant John Charles Fremont. The history of this journey of discovery to the shores of the Pacific is full of romantic incident, and as affording accurate accounts of that great western wilderness which will shortly afford a home for millions of civilised men, is deserving of more notice than it has generally obtained in Europe. Fremont, 'the pathfinder,' was eminently successful in his explorations through the obscure passes of the Rocky Mountains. On one of the topmost peaks of this lofty range, upwards of 13,000 feet above sea-level, he gallantly waved in triumph the national flag, where, as he says, 'never flag waved before.'

The discoveries of Fremont opened the way for settlements, but none, except in an irregular manner, could take place till the territory was organised and surveyed; and these final measures were pushed on by Missourians and others personally acquainted with the capabilities of the unappropriated lands. Among the parties who urged forward the bill for organising the territory, there could hardly fail to be a consciousness that, as Nebraska lay directly north of 36° 30', it was exempted from the contamination of slavery, in virtue of the compromise. But then, was this compromise of abiding effect—was it a compromise at all?

All admitted, what was undeniable, that there was a statute which guaranteed that all lands north of the line 36° 30′, should be consecrated to freedom. This awkward difficulty was got rid of by declaring that the statute was unconstitutional, an interference with the rights of squatter sovereignty. As for there having been a compromise, where was it seen in any valid obligation? It was only a fond tradition, of no binding effect whatsoever. There may have been some mutual concessions among parties when the Missouri bill was passed, more than thirty years ago; but what had the present generation to do with the parliamentary stratagems of a past age? Besides, the compromise measures of 1850 affirm and rest upon the proposition, 'that all questions pertaining to slavery in the territories, and the new states to be formed therefrom, are to be left to the decision of the people residing therein, by their appropriate representatives, to be chosen by them for that purpose.'* According to this view of the subject, the Missouri Compromise of 1820 was over-ridden by Clay's omnibus measure of 1850, which was said to obliterate the line 36° 30′ from the map. Neither branch of congress unanimously adopted so sweeping a doctrine. The progress of the bill, which speedily assumed a form for organising two territories, Kansas and Nebraska, was opposed at every step. Among the more energetic friends of freedom on this occasion, we see the name of Mr Seward (of New York), who, in the course of a long and able speech on the subject, made the following remarks:

'I know there have been states which have endured long, and achieved much, which tolerated slavery; but that was not the slavery of caste, like African slavery.

* *Report of Senate's Committee on Territories, in Reference to Nebraska*, January 1853.

Such slavery tends to demoralise equally the subjected race and the superior one. It has been the absence of such slavery from Europe that has given her nations their superiority over other countries in that hemisphere. Slavery, wherever it exists, begets fear, and fear is the parent of weakness. What is the secret of that eternal, sleepless anxiety in the legislative halls, and even at the firesides of the slave states, always asking new stipulations, new compromises and abrogation of compromises, new assumptions of power and abnegations of power, but fear? It is the apprehension, that, even if safe now, they will not always or long be secure against some invasion or some aggression from the free states. What is the secret of the humiliating part which proud old Spain is acting at this day, trembling between alarms of American intrusion into Cuba on one side, and British dictation on the other, but the fact that she has cherished slavery so long and still cherishes it, in the last of her American colonial possessions? Thus far Kansas and Nebraska are safe, under the laws of 1820, against the introduction of this element of national debility and decline. The bill before us, as we are assured, contains a great principle, a glorious principle; and yet that principle, when fully ascertained, proves to be nothing less than the subversion of that security, not only within the territories of Kansas and Nebraska, but within all the other present and future territories of the United States. Thus it is quite clear that it is not a principle alone that is involved, but that those who crowd this measure with so much zeal and earnestness must expect that either freedom or slavery shall gain something by it in those regions. The case, then, stands thus in Kansas and Nebraska: Freedom may lose, but certainly can gain nothing; while slavery may gain, but as certainly can lose nothing.'

Again, expostulation was useless. The bill passed both branches of the legislature in May 1854, the majority, as customary on similar questions, being swelled by northern Whigs. An act was accordingly framed for organising Kansas and Nebraska as separate territories, with the whole apparatus of local government and legislation. The clause empowering the inhabitants to legalise or reject slavery, is given below.* The two territories being now fairly established, that kind of rush of settlers ensues which has been already pictured. In their choice, Nebraska appears to have been passed over in favour of Kansas, which, lying to the south, on the parallel 36° 30', immediately adjoining Missouri, drew crowds towards it; and, as is well known, became the object of a keen and disorderly competition between the southern slave-holding party and the free-soilers of the north. There was little time to spare. In the Old World, kingdoms and principalities have taken centuries to mature. The greater number, after a thousand years of social organisation, have not yet acquired so much as the capacity to keep order at a public meeting, let alone the power of self-government. Even the British monarchy, with

---

* 'That the constitution, and all the laws of the United States not locally inapplicable, shall have the same force and effect within the territory of Kansas as elsewhere within the United States, *except* the eighth section of the act preparatory to the admission of Missouri into the Union, approved March 6, 1820, which being inconsistent with the principles of non-intervention by congress with slavery in the states and territories, as recognised by the legislation of 1850, commonly called the compromise measures, is hereby declared inoperative and void, it being the true intent and meaning of the act not to legislate slavery into any state or territory, or exclude it therefrom; but to leave the people thereof perfectly free to form and regulate their domestic institutions in their own way, subject only to the constitution of the United States. Provided, that nothing herein contained shall be construed to revive or put in force any law or regulation which may have existed prior to the act of the 6th of March 1820, either protecting, establishing, prohibiting, or abolishing slavery.'

all its appliances, seems to be unable to ripen its ordinary run of colonies under a period of some years —indeed, several of the more elderly of these communities are now, after long tutelage, only beginning to walk alone. The United States contrive to do the thing in a few weeks or months. Kansas was organised on the 30th of May 1854, and on the 29th of November following, it was to elect a delegate to represent it in congress. In the short intermediate period, cities, towns, and voting-places were to receive legal significance; though, as the materials of architecture were principally deals and canvas, this feat was perhaps no great stretch of genius. Previously to its organisation, the region had become a hopeful field of labour to several missionaries connected with one of the divisions of the Methodist body, which is known to have done good service in carrying a knowledge of religion into remote quarters of the Union. It is true these missionaries are often described as being coarse and illiterate, but such, perhaps, are the only men adapted for the rough circumstances that surround them in the backwoods and prairies. Whether to please the parties among whom they minister, or from other motives, it unfortunately happens that these missionaries do not scruple to advocate slavery in union with Scriptural doctrine, and so act as pioneers of a system of brutalising oppression, which is clearly at variance with every principle we are taught to revere. Among those who in this manner had set up their tabernacle in Kansas, was a somewhat renowned personage, the Rev. Tom Johnson, who is described as ultra coarse and presuming—a violent pro-slavery partisan, and a ready tool of those planters in Missouri who had an eye to the fertile plains of the territory. This worthy, whose head-quarters were at a place called the Shawnee Mission, a short way from the frontier, held slaves long before the organisation of Kansas—a circumstance which helped materially forward the plan of introducing and holding slaves on a large scale. Of the Rev. Tom's clerical accomplishments, we possess no record. All we know is, that, located in a hulking brick building at Shawnee Mission, he was a leading man among those who charged themselves with enlightening the Shawnees, Delawares, Kaws, Sacs, Foxes, and other tribes of Indians, some of whom, as our authority states, already possessed in an 'eminent degree the marks of whisky civilisation.'* We do not learn that Tom kept a barrel to aid him in his labours; but that is of no consequence. There were barrels at hand, and they were doing their usually horrid work on the unhappy Indians—a doomed race. The bill opening the territory to white immigration, provided that the natives should not be illegally deprived of their reserves; but no arrangement however humane, short of the annihilation of whisky, could sustain them in their possessions, and, unless removed, they were evidently destined to become beggars and plagues to society. A number, wisely ceding their lands on reasonable terms, were transferred to localities at a suitable distance, where they remain till a fresh wave of white immigration overtakes them.

As the aborigines, half-demoralised, gloomily clear out, the whites pour in; land-offices are opened; 'claims' begin to dot the face of the country; and the cluster of ugly buildings at Shawnee Mission, becomes a rallying-point for the settlers. We are to view Kansas in this transition state in July 1854, when the contest between pro-slavery and anti-slavery emigrants comes distinctly into notice. According to the account

* *The Conquest of Kansas by Missouri and her Allies.* By W. Phillips. Boston. 1856.

of the pro-slavery Missourians, they were stung by newspaper reports that great bands of New Englanders would soon be on their way to introduce free institutions into Kansas. About this time, several joint-stock concerns were formed in the free states for this avowed purpose. One of them, called the New-England Emigrant Aid Company, with a capital stock of 5,000,000 dollars, was legalised by an act of incorporation from the legislature of Massachusetts. The plan proposed by the company was this: Agents were to buy lands in Kansas, and sell them in lots to immigrants, until the territory was organised as a free state; then, all funds being realised, and a dividend declared, the agents were to select a fresh field of operations in order to organise another free state. In short, it was a grand device to give free institutions to all the new territories, one after the other; and if unopposed, there could have been little doubt of its success. These projects alarmed the Missourians—at least, such is their story. It is, however, quite as clear that the pro-slavery men were, from the first, equally on the alert; and we are to conclude that both parties had some time previously determined to run a race for the territory. The committee of congress which afterwards investigated the matter, states in its report, that 'within a few days after the organic law was passed, and as soon as its passage could be known on the border, leading citizens of Missouri crossed into the territory, held squatter meetings, and then returned to their homes. Among the resolutions are the following: That we will afford protection to no abolitionist as a settler of this territory: that we recognise the institution of slavery as already existing in this territory, and advise slaveholders to introduce their property as early as possible.' Then, early in July, a meeting of an association, having the same object in view, takes place at Westport, and resolves that it will hold itself in readiness to remove any and all emigrants who go into Kansas under the auspices of the Northern Emigrant Aid Societies. Thus, two opposite parties were distinctly pitted against each other. Had the Missourians confined themselves to the peaceful settlement of planters and slaves, no fault could be found with them *under the constitution,* however much, on moral grounds, we might have lamented their aggressions. But the pro-slaveryites went a step beyond their constitutional rights. Not contenting themselves with a plan of peaceful emigration, they resolved, as we have seen, to gain their ends by violence. One excuse for their outrages is, that in giving a charter of incorporation to the New-England Emigrant Aid Company, the legislature of Massachusetts committed a trespass on the constitution; because no state is warranted in doing anything which will operate on the institutions of another state. For anything we can tell, this may have been an indiscreet and federally unlawful act; but, if such were the case, there was surely legal redress before the supreme courts of the Union. Nothing, in a word, can justify the Missourians in having armed themselves to oppose the settlement of the northern emigrants; and for this they stand condemned in the estimation of all right-thinking persons in Europe and America.

A number of quietly disposed emigrants had begun to spread themselves on the banks of the Kaw, when they heard that they were to be attacked. They were discomposed, but not frightened, and stood their ground. It seems to be customary to give the inhabitants of many of the states certain nicknames, by which they are generally known. The natives of Illinois are called *Suckers;* those of Indiana, *Hoosiers;* and the Missourians receive the unpleasant name of *Pukes*. Well, the story ran in Kansas that the Pukes were coming, and soon a squad of them did make their appearance. Phillips, whose work presents the only intelligible narrative of the Kansas troubles that has fallen in our way, gives a graphic account of the Pukes, or 'border ruffians.' They are of several kinds. Those of the unadulterated type, are decided characters. 'Most of them,' he says, 'have been over the plains several times; if they have not been over the plains, the probability is, they have served through the war in Mexico, or seen "a deal of trouble in Texas," or at least run up and down the Missouri river often enough to catch imitative inspiration from the catfish aristocracy. I have often wondered where all the hard customers on the Missouri frontier come from. They seem to have congregated here by some law of gravity unexplainable. Perhaps the *easy* exercise of judicial authority in frontier countries may explain their fancy for them. Amongst these worthies, a man is estimated by the amount of whisky he can drink; and if he is so indiscreet as to admit he "drinks no liquor," he is set down as a dangerous character, and shunned accordingly. Imagine a fellow, tall, slim, but athletic, with yellow complexion, hairy faced, with a dirty flannel shirt, red, or blue, or green, a pair of common-place, but dark-coloured pants, tucked into an uncertain altitude by a leather-belt, in which a dirty-handled bowie-knife is stuck rather ostentatiously, an eye slightly whisky red, and teeth the colour of a walnut. Such is your border ruffian of the lowest type. His body might be a compound of gutta-percha, Johnny-cake, and badly smoked bacon; his spirit, the *refined* part, old Bourbon, "double rectified;" but there is every shade of the border ruffian. Your judicial ruffian, for instance, is a gentleman; that is, as much of a gentleman as he can be without transgressing on his more purely legitimate character of border ruffian. As "occasional imbibing" is not a sin, his character at home is irreproachable; and when he goes abroad into the territory, for instance, he does not *commit* any act of outrage, or vote himself, but after "aiding and comforting" those who do, returns, feeling every inch a *gentleman*. Then there are your less conservative border-ruffian *gentlemen*. They are not so nice in distinctions, and, so far from objecting, rather like to take a hand themselves; but they dress like gentlemen, and are so after a fashion. Between these and the first-mentioned large class, there is every shade and variety; but it takes the whole of them to make an effective brigade; and *then* it is not perfect without a barrel of whisky. The two *gentlemanly* classes of ruffians are so for political effect, or because they fancy it is their interest. The lower class are pro-slavery ruffians, merely because it is the prevalent kind of rascality; the inference is, that they would engage in any other affair in which an equal amount of whisky might be drunk, or as great an aggregate of rascality be perpetrated. Such was the kind of customers who presented themselves to the astonished gaze of the early citizens of Lawrence, while it spread its tent-like butterfly wings, just emerging from its chrysalis state, on the banks of the Kaw.'

A description of the arrival of the Pukes is given with picturesque effect. 'They came in wagons, and were truly an "army with banners." Every wagon appeared to be supplied with a piece of cloth, which was patched something to represent a star, or other more mysterious border-ruffian symbols, and also a jug of whisky. They had a fiddler or two with them, their nearest approximation to "martial music." They might be styled the shot-gun, or backwoods' rifle, brigade. In a representation of the *Forty Thieves*, they would have been invaluable, with their grim visages, their tipsy expression, and, above all, their oaths and unapproachable swagger. As the first detachment only numbered eighty men, they took to the north side of the ravine which runs through town, this being the Rubicon between them and the Yankees. When there, they proceeded to swagger and drink, and shoot at marks, and swear by all that was good and bad that they would exterminate all the Yankee abolitionists that dare come to Kansas. Towards the evening of the day they came, a reinforcement of some twenty-five more arrived; but they either did not deem themselves strong enough yet, or had adopted some plan of operations requiring delay.' Some diplomatic intercourse follows, but there was as yet no fighting. The New Englanders would not give way, and ultimately the border ruffians retired.

The two principal officers appointed by the president to initiate the territorial government, were A. H. Reeder, as governor, and S. D. Lecompte, as chief-justice. Reeder was evidently not the man for the situation. He arrived in October, and the election of a delegate to congress took place, as has been said, on the 29th of November. At this election, Whitfield, the pro-slavery candidate, was returned; but the majority in his favour was increased by 1729 illegal votes, given by bands of men who crossed the frontier from Missouri—another act totally unjustifiable. The report of the committee of congress declares it to have been 'a systematic invasion from an adjoining state, by which large numbers of illegal votes were cast in remote and sparse settlements, for the avowed purpose of extending slavery into the territory,' and which, 'even though it did not change the result of the election, was a crime of great magnitude. Its immediate effect was to further excite the people of the northern states, induce acts of retaliation, and exasperate the actual settlers against their neighbours in Missouri.' *

Dire events followed, but we must leave an account of them to next chapter.

* According to Phillips, the intruders represented only a faction in Missouri; large numbers in that state repudiated their proceedings, but from the terrorism that prevailed, were unable to interfere. 'Although,' says this authority, 'Missouri is a slave state, slavery is chiefly to be found in a few counties, and even there the large majority of the white men are not slave-owners. They are men who have come from all states of the Union, some of them enterprising business-men, who, in advancing their private interests, have still a reasonable pride in those liberties and privileges guaranteed to them by the constitution, and bought by the blood of the early patriots. But freedom of speech is suppressed as thoroughly as ever it was in the days of the Inquisition. Not only is the subject of slavery itself interdicted, but all opinions growing out of it, or that might haply endanger it, are forbidden.' An organisation of secret lodges compels silence and passive obedience. . 'An election is to be carried; and if there is not a sufficient number of rowdies to engage in it, from a natural love of mischief, and an acquired love of liquor, why, more respectable men must go. And if they do not go, they must at least pay the expenses of those who do. . . . . Not a whisper must be breathed against this cruel taxation, or else the luckless wight, whose love of principle (or parsimony) made him object, would be subjected to a loss of caste, to which the condition of an Indian Pariah is a happy one. The following speech, delivered by General Stringfellow, in St Joseph, Missouri, at a public meeting where he was sustained and indorsed, will tell something of the story: "I tell you to mark every scoundrel among you who is the least tainted with abolitionism or free-soilism, and exterminate him. Neither give nor take quarter from the . . . . rascals. I propose to mark them in this house, and on the present occasion ; so you may crush them out. To those who have qualms of conscience as to violating laws, state or national, the time has come when such impositions must be disregarded, as your rights and property are in danger. I advise you, one and all, to enter every election district in Kansas, in defiance of Reeder and his vile myrmidons, and vote at the point of the bowie-knife and revolver. Neither give nor take quarter, as the cause demands it. It is enough that the slaveholding interest wills it, from which there is no appeal."'—*Phillips*, p. 47.

The election of a delegate to congress, from the territory of Kansas, in November 1854, was followed, as has been said, by dire events. The free settlers were indignant at the unauthorised voting of pro-slavery men from Missouri, and the Missourians endeavoured by acts of outrage to intimidate and expel the settlers. Violence, however, had not yet attained its climax. The great struggle was to take place on the 30th of March 1855, when the inhabitants were to choose a legislature. Preparatory to this event, Governor Reeder caused a census to be taken of the population, which was found to consist of 8501 souls. This number included the unenfranchised part of the community, 242 slaves and 151 free negroes; those entitled to vote amounting to 2905.

As the great day approached, parties of Missourians entered the territory, and planted themselves at every polling-place, with the avowed design of voting for candidates who would make Kansas a slave state. As many as 5000 of these desperadoes, equipped with arms, and bringing tents and provisions, thus took their ground, resolved to commit a grossly illegal act, by representing themselves as actual inhabitants of the territory. As there is not usually any register of voters in the States, where elections are often a kind of scramble—the very sheriffs, on such occasions, lending themselves to party purposes—it is not difficult for bands of resolute individuals to carry everything as they please. Even in the city of New York, at the last election, as is stated by the local press, parties of rowdies floated from polling-place to polling-place, and cast votes at them all, in order to return their favourite candidate. How much more easily could such infamous proceedings occur in the wildernesses of Kansas!

Well, the election takes place. Notwithstanding threats of personal violence, the settlers came pretty freely forward; but of what avail against the host of intruders? On examination, it was found that the number of legal voters was 1310, and of illegal voters, 4908. With the exception of two, all the members returned were pro-slavery men, and a number of them were residents in Missouri. It being the duty of the governor to receive the returns, and grant certificates to enable members to assume office, Reeder, after, as is alleged, investigating each case, set aside the election in seven disputed districts, thus creating two vacancies in the council, and nine in the house of representatives. He issued a certificate, besides, to one member of council and one member of the house, not the individuals whom the judges of the election had returned. To all the remainder, consisting of eleven councilmen, and seventeen representatives, he granted certificates. On his ordering a new election to be held on the 24th of May for filling up the vacancies, the pro-slavery party broke into a storm of indignation. They declared that no special election was valid under the organic law; they resolved to disown the authority of the present one, and vowed vengeance against Reeder and all who adhered to him. Without waiting for the new election, the governor, in April, issued his proclamation, summoning the legislature to meet at Pawnee City—a cluster of tents and deals about a hundred miles from the frontier —on the 2d of July.

At the May election, there was little disturbance,

and the free-soilers had almost everything their own way; the result being the return of a number of new members, to whom the governor granted certificates. There were now, as we may say, double returns, some apparently valid, others the reverse. No proceedings, however, were founded on this point till the assemblage of the two houses, when, on the third day of the session, a committee made a report respecting disputed elections. Not to go into tiresome minutiæ, the result of the inquiry was, to deprive of his seat one of the members whom the governor had certified in March, and to turn out six members certified under the election in May—the effect of the whole being to restore affairs to nearly that position in which they had been placed by the outrageous intrusion of the Missourians in March. Reeder, it may be presumed, had now an opportunity of repudiating a legislature so vitiated by its own act, but, as previously hinted, though a man of good intentions, he was scarcely fitted for controlling the wild democracy over whom he was called to rule. One of the earliest projects started in the house of representatives was the removal of the seat of legislature to Shawnee Mission, near the borders of Missouri; and a bill to this effect was sent to the governor, who, on the 6th of July, returned it with a message declining to sanction the proposed change. His reason was, that the legislature had transcended its authority in adopting this particular measure; but in making this communication, he distinctly recognised the council and house of representatives as constituting the legislature of the territory of Kansas. As may be supposed, the legislative body paid no attention to the governor's objections, and accordingly removed, on the 16th of July, to a schoolhouse at Shawnee Mission. Still, the governor by messages respecting bills continued to recognise the authority of the legislature, although at the same time, on the 21st of July, he declared that, by the act of removal, the two houses were dissolved, and henceforth he suspended all intercourse with them. We are conscious that these are dry details, but being gathered chiefly from a report of congress respecting the struggle in Kansas, and freed from party exaggerations, they throw a useful light over what has become a question of deep interest connected with the progress of slavery. Up to the point we have reached, the Missouri intruders were decidedly in the wrong; the denunciations in their newspapers and speeches at the public meetings were atrocious—language which we could not possibly transfer to these pages. But unfortunately, Reeder, in whose hands was the destiny of Kansas, compromised freedom. His recognition of the corrupt legislature on the 21st of July, was a grave blunder; for in a legal point of view (as we humbly assume), no subsequent repudiation of that body could deprive it of an authority he had already acknowledged. The false position taken by Reeder was greedily seized hold of by his antagonists, who, as an explanation of his conduct, alleged that his preference for Pawnee arose from the fact of his having town-lots to dispose of in that quarter. Whatever truth may be in the scandal circulated on the occasion, there can be no doubt, if we are to believe Phillips, that Shawnee was a much more agreeable place of meeting than Pawnee. 'At the Mission, the legislature were at home; that is, they were nearly so. It was only one mile from the Missouri line, and four miles from Westport. Hacks left the Mission every evening, on the adjournment, taking the members to Westport, and brought them back in the morning. And such splendid junketings and racketings these fellows had! A due supply of whisky was brought in bottles and jugs each morning, in order to keep the legislature *in spirits* during the long summer days.'

Having set to work, the *Bogus* legislature, as this body is usually designated, speedily produced a code of laws connected with 'slave property,' such as the world has not seen for many a day. The following are a few of the penalties: To any person concerned in raising an insurrection among slaves, or free coloured persons—death. To any person who shall entice, decoy, or carry away any slave from the territory —death, or imprisonment for ten years with hard labour. To any person who shall entice or persuade a slave to escape from his master—imprisonment for ten years with hard labour. To any person resisting an officer who attempts to arrest an escaped slave— imprisonment with hard labour for two years. The following sections are too good to abridge:

'If any person print, write, introduce into, or circulate, or cause to be brought into, written, printed, or circulated, or shall knowingly aid or assist in bringing into, printing, publishing, or circulating within this territory, any book, paper, pamphlet, magazine, handbill, or circular containing any statements, arguments, opinions, sentiment, doctrine, advice, or innuendo calculated to produce a disorderly, dangerous, or rebellious disaffection among the slaves of the territory, or to induce such slaves to escape from the service of their masters, or to resist their authority, he shall be guilty of felony, and be punished by imprisonment at hard labour for a term not less than five years. If any free person, by speaking or writing, assert or maintain that persons have not the right to hold slaves in this territory, or shall introduce into this territory, print, publish, write, circulate, or cause to be introduced into the territory, written, printed, published, and circulated in this territory any book, paper, magazine, pamphlet, or circular, containing any denial of the right of persons to hold slaves in this territory, such person shall be deemed guilty of felony, and punished by imprisonment at hard labour for a term of not less than two years. No person who is conscientiously opposed to holding slaves, or who does not admit the right to hold slaves in this territory, shall sit as a juror on the trial of any prosecution for any violation of any of the sections of this act.' This extraordinary code was subscribed by J. H. Stringfellow as Speaker of the House, and Thomas Johnson (the Rev. Tom), President of the Council.

The bills passed by the Bogus legislature being, as a matter of form, submitted to Reeder for his sanction, he transmitted a message in reply, stating that his opinion remained unchanged respecting the illegality of that body, but that independently of this fact, he had received official intimation that his functions as governor were withdrawn. The latter part of this reply was probably anticipated; for the legislature had memorialised the president to remove the governor from office; nor can we feel any surprise at his dismissal. Will it be credited—his message just alluded to (August 16) was still addressed 'To the honourable the members of the council and house of representatives of the territory of Kansas'*—an acknowledgment of their authority at variance with his repeated declarations, and greatly calculated to complicate the whole question. Amidst these difficulties, the Bogus legislature obtained an opinion from Judge Lecompte, to the effect, that the bills passed would receive the force of law without the signature of the governor, and so they appear to have actually come into operation.

* *Majority Report of Committee of Congress.* March 1856.

Reeder, who now withdrew into private life, was replaced by Governor Shannon, who was declared to be 'sound on the goose'—that is, in favour of slavery in the territory—and who, in general character, was no improvement on his predecessor. Indignant at being subjected to laws which they believed to rest on no proper authority, and exposed to personal sufferings from the Missourians, the citizens of Kansas spent the summer of 1855 in a state of extreme agitation. The proper means for redress lay in a calm appeal to congress. They did memorialise that body on the subject of their grievances; and ultimately a committee inquired into and reported on the subject at voluminous length. Without, however, waiting for the action of the supreme government, the citizens of Kansas held mass-meetings denunciatory of their oppressors, and went the extreme length of appointing a governor, C. Robinson, to 'occupy the executive chair of the new state of Kansas.' Under this official took place an entirely new organisation of the territory —alleged by the parties concerned to be exactly in terms of the constitution, but considered by the supreme government as totally irregular and inadmissible. The people in the several districts elected delegates, with perfect seriousness, to constitute a convention, or rival body to the Bogus legislature; and on the meeting of the assembly on the 19th of September at Topeka, a message was delivered from 'Governor Robinson,' which would have done no discredit to the president of the United States.

Looking at the acts and resolutions of the Topeka convention, it was decidedly the better legislature of the two. Considering the nature of its materials, and the circumstances calling it into existence, one cannot but feel amazed at the cool and business-like way in which it set aside the whole proceedings of the Bogus assembly, drew up a constitution, organised committees on education and other affairs, and appointed an executive for the territory. None but an American, however, can do justice to its character. 'This constitutional convention,' says Phillips, ' was by far the most respectable body of men in point of talent, that was convened in Kansas; indeed, it would have compared favourably with legislative bodies anywhere. Talent, and the weak vanity which apes it, were there; true virtue, and a more plastic school of morality; patriotism, and number-one-ism; outside influence, and a lobby; sober, staid, business habits; brandy, temperance, whisky, prayers by the chaplain, profanity and oyster-suppers. It lacked none of the great essentials.' Taken all in all, it was an honourable body, with the usual sprinkling of skilful politicians, who knew how to indoctrinate an infant community with the principles of party manœuvring.

There were now two rival parliaments in Kansas, each thundering forth laws; but of what use are all the laws in the world, if there is nobody to execute them? Even in despotic countries, it is the people who control the people. The Bogus legislature of Kansas was an exotic, the governor an exotic, and the judges and sheriffs exotics: the people repudiated the whole concern, and defied them. There being, properly speaking, neither law nor government, and outrages being of daily occurrence, the settlers got up secret military organisations, the chief of these being called the Kansas Legion—a kind of *Vehmgericht*, holding mysterious meetings, and the members of which recognised each other by peculiar signs. To counteract these movements, and aid the Bogus legislature, the pro-slavery men held what they called a 'Law and Order Convention' at Leavenworth on the 14th of November; and of this professed auxiliary of the constituted authorities, Governor Shannon was appointed president. From this period may be dated the condition of anarchy in Kansas. At all points, there was open defiance between the two parties. Of the fights, slaughterings, burning of houses, destruction and stealing of property, and personal outrages of every kind, we are fortunately spared from giving any account, as ample details of the atrocities committed by the border ruffians have been made widely known, and more particularly as that greatest atrocity of all, the burning and sacking of the city of Lawrence, in May 1856, must be fresh in every one's recollection. By Mrs Robinson, wife of Governor Robinson, who was carried away a prisoner, a circumstantial and graphic account of the troubles in Kansas has been given to the world.

In July 1856, the Topeka convention was brought to a termination by order of Colonel Sumner,* at the head of a troop of dragoons, despatched by the supreme government to suppress the insurrections in the territory. With the interruption of the free-state convention, the seizure of some prisoners, and the occupancy of Kansas by the federal forces, the territory was substantially handed over to the Missourians. How far the president was justified in sending an army into Kansas, has been matter of much angry discussion; his proceedings in this respect, while ostensibly designed to keep the peace, had the effect of vindicating the conduct of the Missourian intruders, and leaving the actual settlers helpless. The subject, it will be recollected, brought congress to a dead-lock at the end of August 1856, when an appropriation for the army required to be voted. On this occasion, the members

* Meetings of the Topeka convention took place subsequently, but not to any good purpose.

of the House of Representatives from the free states had it in their power to stop the supplies, and thus withdraw the army from Kansas. This grand chance of historical renown was not embraced. By a majority of 101 to 98, the vote for appropriation was ultimately carried—21 members from free states being numbered in the majority.

Under Governor Geary, Kansas has latterly been tranquil, and things may be said to be mending. But the laws of the Bogus legislature, which impose and bolster up slavery, remain in force. It is only barely possible that they may be abolished, and a new order of things introduced by congress. Some New York newspapers, we observe, are recommending free-state emigrants to proceed to the territory, which presents cheap and fertile lands for settlement; and, considering the mighty stake at issue, we are not surprised that fresh attempts should be made to pour in an independent class of settlers. He would ill understand the nature of the struggle in Kansas, who supposed it to relate solely to the freedom of that territory. No doubt, that was the great and proximate object; but when we say that by making Kansas free, slavery would be checked in its north-western flank, and receive a severe blow throughout its whole system, the character of that desperate life-and-death struggle, which we have faintly portrayed, will perhaps be better understood. By way of a final settlement, possibly, some one on whom has dropped the mantle of Henry Clay, may propose a new Compromise!

In judging of past events in this unhappy territory, a sense of impartiality obliges us to say that all parties were in the wrong. Congress committed in the first place a grievous wrong, by instituting squatter sovereignty in direct opposition to the Missouri Compromise. Pierce seems to have done wrong throughout, in his invariable leaning to the pro-slavery party, and so encouraging their aggressions. Then, as regards the two local parties, wrong was met with wrong, illegality by illegality. The intrusions of the border ruffians were in every point of view iniquitous; but the free-soil settlers, though grossly insulted and oppressed, did surely wrong in inaugurating an irregular legislative convention, and in trying to support their plans by secret military organisations. As for Reeder, the central figure in the group of wrong-doers, he, by his incorrigible folly, rendered confusion worse confounded —a fine instance of what mischief may be done by good easy men, when placed in circumstances demanding vigour of character. For all these complications of wrong, of which no one can yet see the end, the more peaceful and honestly disposed immigrants to Kansas paid a heavy penalty. Their sufferings were acute, their losses ruinous. Of the deplorable condition to which their agricultural operations were reduced, we could advance no more convincing proof than that which above all things shocks the sensibility of an American—*white* women were seen labouring in the fields!

Squatter sovereignty!—shall it exist or not, is the question which for half a century has perplexed and demoralised American statesmanship, and will do so apparently for some time to come. Calhoun is said to have been the first to use the term 'squatter sovereignty' in joke, though no joke has it proved to congress; but Cass is alleged to have had the high merit of giving it a place in serious parliamentary nomenclature, and so conferring upon it an air of official respectability. We do not absolutely pledge ourselves as to the authorship of either of these distinguished statesmen; nor does it much matter. Squatter sovereignty is no new thing. We have referred to it again and again as the alleged right of the inhabitants of the newly organised territories of the Union to make choice of their own institutions. How that choice is for the most part a foregone conclusion, as regards slavery, is already explained. An early rush of planters with their slaves usually settles the business, before the more slow-moving and freedom-loving emigrants enter on the scene. Yet, the fiction is still contended for in congress, that the inhabitants are entitled to exercise precisely the same right of assuming or rejecting slavery as are the citizens of any of the constituted states.

People who do not keep quite abreast of great social questions, probably imagine that the contest about slavery in the United States refers to emancipation or non-emancipation. Except by the inconsiderable party of abolitionists, the struggle has not got within 'a long chalk' of this ultimatum. The past and present subject of debate, is what is to be done with the territories, which are from time to time absorbed into the Union. The South, which has the knack of carrying statesmen and presidents along with it—no matter where these personages are 'raised' —argues strongly in favour of squatter sovereignty; for the good reason, that it can fabricate pro-slavery squatters to any desired amount. The North, on the other hand, which talks heroically about freedom in its Faneuil Halls, its Tabernacles, and what not, and is clear that at least all territories on the northern side of 36° 30' should be for ever free from slavery, cuts a poor figure when it comes to voting. In plain terms, it allows itself to be mystified—sends, among a few brilliant exceptions, so many self-interested persons to congress, that all 'who are not identified with cotton or democracy are naturally disgusted' *— and thus, to end the matter, the South gets pretty nearly always its own way.

Ever since the battle of the territories began, nearly forty years ago, there has been a continual reckoning of gains and losses between South and North. On our conscience, we believe that the question of slavery has never, as a general rule, been seriously entertained by the great northern orators in congress. The thing which was really fought for—as, for example, in the magnificent speeches of Webster—was political power. If the South, with the peculiar energy it has usually employed, were to secure a disproportionately large number of states, the North would relatively sink in its member-creating capacity; and losing in members, it would lose in chances of place as well as of the

* *Whig Policy Analysed and Illustrated.* By Josiah Quincy. Boston, 1856.

many good things which issue from the federal treasury. Unless one is pretty well 'posted up' in the history of these party manœuvres, he can hardly comprehend the actual merits of the squatter sovereignty discussions.

Slavery, once simply a social and seemingly temporary evil, has, through the course of events, of which we have presented a summary, become a great political institute, within which is intrenched an oligarchy that holds the balance of power, and is, in effect, *the* government. Undoubtedly, the primary cause of this preponderance is the constitution of the United States, which is eminently conservative of slavery, and, as usually interpreted, has afforded reasons for greatly extending this odious institution. In that constitutional arrangement alone, whereby slaves form an element in apportioning the ratio of representative population, a ground was laid for the political aggrandisement of the South. As formerly stated, three-fifths of all the slaves in the United States are numbered in the constituency for the House of Representatives, though not one of them has a vote. Three out of every five slaves in the South, are thus equivalent to three freemen in the North; and practically, by this singular method of making up a constituency, the South gains thirty votes in the House of Representatives beyond what it ought properly to be entitled to have.

It is worthy of remark, however, that, notwithstanding this remarkable advantage, the South is not able to keep pace with northern constituencies. By the last decennial census, on which the present representation is based, while the free states contribute 145 members, the slave states return no more than 90. How, then, being in such a minority, is the South able to exert so extraordinary an influence in the national legislature? The explanation involves some strange disclosures. In the first place, the South uniformly acts with an *esprit du corps* totally wanting in the North. The constituency of the slave states is, in point of fact, narrowed to about 350,000 slave-owners, in whom power is entirely reposed; the surplus of southern white population being little better than a nonentity. A body so limited acts with a vigour and unity not to be attained by the many millions of northern freemen. Throughout the South, free labour is dishonourable, and the business of life is politics: the universal consideration is the attainment and retention of power. The North, on the contrary, is a hive of industry, in which there is little time to devote to political stratagems, and unfortunately the people, generally, are so much under the dominion of material interests, as well as prejudices respecting colour, as to be easily misled by deceptive party representations.

Accustomed as we are to associate slavery and its multifarious horrors with the doings of the South, one is apt to neglect the important truth, that but for the selfish compromises of the North, slavery must long since have been extinct. No fact has been more conclusively proved than that the existence of this monster evil depends on territorial aggression. Seclude it within a certain circle, and it will inevitably perish. Slavery is synonymous with *waste*. It is a waste of human beings, a waste of means, a waste of land, a waste of moral feeling—everything deteriorates in connection with it. As an institution, it has drawn its vitality from the rich lands lying beyond the borders of the old thirteen states. The most striking evidence of its ruinous effects on land, as well as morals, is given by Mr Olmsted in his two dispassionately written works on the slave states. In the latest of these productions, *A Journey through Texas*, he speaks of that frequent and melancholy spectacle in the older slave states—'an abandoned plantation of "worn-out" fields, with its little village of dwellings, now a home only for wolves and vultures.' 'This,' he adds, 'but indicates a large class of observations, by which I hold myself justified in asserting that the natural elements of wealth in the soil of Texas will have been more exhausted in ten years, and with them the rewards offered by Providence to labour will have been more lessened than, without slavery, would have been the case in two hundred. Do not think that I use round numbers carelessly. After two hundred years' occupation of similar soils by a free labouring community, I have seen no such evidences of waste, as in Texas, after ten years of slavery. And indications of the same kind I have observed, not isolated, but general, in every slave state but two—which I have seen only in parts yet scarcely at all settled. Moreover, I have seen similar phenomena following slavery in other countries and other climates.'

The effects of this wastefulness of land, are of national concern. Present existence is secured by drawing on future resources. To after generations, bread, meat, cotton, and other articles will all be enhanced in cost by the present system of territorial exhaustion. 'I consider,' adds this writer, 'that slavery is no less disastrous in its effects on industry —no less destructive to wealth. The laws and forces sustaining it, where it has been long established, may become a temporary necessity, as poisons are to the life of some unfortunate invalids. But laws intended to extend its field of improvidence are unjust, cruel, and oppressive.' If slavery be so ruinous, why should it be continued? It is tolerably evident that the buying of labourers, instead of hiring them, must be a most extravagant method of cultivating lands. Olmsted shews how capital is needlessly absorbed by investments in slaves, and that on this account alone, the South deprives itself of vast means of improvement. But independently of the profits derived by Virginians in raising and selling slave-stock, there are powerful reasons why slavery is maintained and contended for.

The first of these reasons is the inordinate love of power. Reared in the uncontrolled exercise of authority, the slave-owner will submit to many inconveniences and even loss of profit, rather than tolerate what he considers the arrogance of an independent labourer. To ask a servant to do a thing instead of ordering him, is intolerable. The idea of hired labourers presuming to have rights, is repugnant to southern notions. Those who degrade themselves with labour, are bound to submit to any kind of treatment. The reckless homicide of a waiter at Washington by a member of congress from Alabama, in the spring of 1856, was, for example, justified by southern newspapers, on the ground that it was proper to teach free labourers their place. Another reason for sustaining slavery, is the status which is derived from the possession of negro property. The owning of even one slave raises a person in southern society, although the possessor of this miserable piece of property is under the necessity of hiring it out for his own subsistence. Addressing a southern man, Olmsted says: 'It is fashionable with you to own slaves, as it is with the English to own land, with the Arabs, horses; and as beads and vermilion have a value among the Indians which seems to us absurd, so, among you, has the power of commanding the service of slaves. Consequently, you are willing to pay a price for it which, to one not educated as you have been, seems absurdly high. Nor are you more likely to dispense with slaves when you have it in your power to possess them, than the Chinese with their fashion of the queue, Turks with their turban, or Englishmen with their hats.'

Wrong in principle, and in all respects ineconomical, as compared with free labour, slavery is on all hands acknowledged to exist only by fraud and violence, by disregard of the rights of citizens, by suppressing freedom of discussion and freedom of election, by preventing general education, by interrupting and annoying commerce, by exhausting lands, dishonouring industry, checking public improvements, degrading the national character, and, in short, by establishing an almost universal terrorism, unworthy of a free people. The dexterity with which these enormities has been sustained, is exceedingly marvellous. A few facts must be plainly stated. Practically a despotism, the great slaveholding interest, with far-sighted policy, professes those extreme principles of democracy which are upheld by the larger proportion of northern citizens—much as if the high conservative body in England were, for party purposes, to declare for extreme radicalism. Northern men, on the other hand, seek to conciliate the South, for the sake of selfish interests. The doctrine that high protective duties are an essential element of national prosperity, though long since exploded by political economists, is still current in the northern states of the Union. Doubtless, it is only through the efficacy of such protective duties as 30 per cent., that certain northern manufacturers can keep open their establishments; and we may assume that if these restrictions were removed, much misdirected capital would flow into more natural channels, and produce results more advantageous to all parties. Northern manufacturers, however, being the immediate gainers by so preposterous a system of protection, cling as closely to the privilege of taxing the community as ever did the landowners of Great Britain by their restrictions on the free import of food. Such prepossessions could meet with no response in the South, but for the necessity of buying party support. All the clothing, shoes, hats, and other articles required on southern plantations, are imported coastwise from northern manufacturers; so that, in reality, the South taxes itself in an enormous sum annually, in purchasing dear northern goods. 'Up to the present moment,' says an American writer, 'the North has been a commercial and equal partner with the South in all the material values or pecuniary results produced by slavery. In the first place, the great southern staples, cotton, tobacco, and rice, with their vast valuation, constituting virtually the commercial currency between America and Europe, have mostly passed through the hands of northern merchants and factors, enriching them with lucrative profits. Then, slavery rendered the southern states dependent upon the North for all the manufactured articles they used; from parlour books to kitchen brooms; from beaver-hats for the master to the coarsest chip-hats for the slave; from penknives to ploughs. Nearly all the goods they used were either manufactured or imported for them by the North. Their teas, coffees, and other foreign productions either came to them through New York, Philadelphia, or Boston, or were brought to them direct from across the sea in northern ships. The factories and ships of the eastern states and the fertile prairie lands of the west, teemed with the industrial activities which these important staples employed and rewarded. What three millions of slaves grew under the lash in the South, made a continuous and profitable business for at least twice that number of freemen in the North. The latter, by that species of compromise for which it has been distinguished, grasped at the lion's share of the dividends of this commercial partnership. It coveted to sell to the southern states, far more than it purchased from them. If they would only consent to a high protective tariff, which would give their market for manufactures exclusively to the North, anti-slavery agitation in the free states should be put down and extinguished. The mobbing of "abolition agitators" in Boston, New York, Philadelphia, and other northern cities, was a part of this business transaction—a small instalment of the purchase-price of *protection.** The case then stands thus: the South pretends to be democratic, to gain northern votes; and the North sells itself for public money. Or, to come to the subject in hand—the South votes for Protection, and the North in return votes for Slavery.

Slavery, at least on its present footing, may therefore be said to exist, in some degree, on commercial protection. It is not to be supposed that the South is unanimous in submitting to this thraldom to northern interests. At the risk of breaking up the mutual understanding, southern orators and newspapers have strongly advocated free-trade with Europe, and numerous have been the projects to establish southern harbours, shipping, and commerce—all, of course, impracticable, on account of want of capital as well as want of business calculations and habits. Did the South really find it safe to break with the North, it would, perhaps, with its legislative influence find little difficulty in forcing free-trade measures; and from present appearances, acts of congress may take this direction.

* *Plan of Brotherly Copartnership.* By Elihu Burritt.

It can admit of little doubt, that as protection is relaxed, so will a material cement between North and South be dissolved—an event so far favourable to the interests of freedom. But as long as the principles of democracy are in the ascendant, the anti-slavery party will not have great cause to rejoice. According to the confession of political faith, demonstrated in recent elections, democracy signifies the vindication of squatter sovereignty, the boundless extension of the Union, and consequently the illimitable addition of new slave states. Can such principles be carried out? Are they not of a character with all that has been tolerated since the acquisition of Louisiana? It is confidently expected that the rising and somewhat formidable opposition presented by the republican party, will interpose to prevent the further spread of slavery. But this, we fear, is only one of those idle expectations, with which the less sophisticated part of the nation has been long deceitfully amused. The South has many methods of disarming opposition. It can threaten dissolution of the Union, and that few can endure; for devotion to the Union is a predominant sentiment with almost every American. By its vigorous action, the South can retain possession of power, and so effectually does it swamp the majority of free-state votes in congress by means at its disposal, that it laughs to scorn the still unpopular efforts of disunionists and abolitionists.

Referring to the change of sentiment on the subject of slavery in the North, Mr Quincy, whom we have already quoted, shews how, step by step, the principles of freedom have sunk under party influences. Soon after the adoption of the constitution, he says, 'a change of feeling began to spread in the free states, in which, from envy, jealousy, rivalry, ambition, and other passions, parties arose, of which the slaveholders had the tact to avail themselves. .... It was the mutual interest which resulted from the alliance between slavery and democracy, that at first softened, and in time changed, in Massachusetts, the early, inherent detestation of negro slavery. This change did not extend beyond the democratic party. But after the lapse of twenty or thirty years, another element of slaveholders' influence was introduced. In the course of these years, the profits arising from the cultivation of cotton in the southern states, changed the opinion of the rich planters concerning the evil of slavery, which at first began there to be considered as a good, and then subsequently as a chief good. A like change, contemporaneously, came over the free states, in certain localities, where cotton-spinning and cotton-weaving began to be a source of wealth, and consequently of political power. This interest acquired strength with time and prosperity, and began to be a predominating influence, about the period the Whig party was formed, constituting in truth the chief part of its cement. It was formed out of the broken materials of the old parties, which time and circumstances had dissolved, and was composed of recently fledged politicians, with a mixture of some democrats and some federalists, who joined the new party, not because its principles were to their mind, but because it was the best in the field. It took the name of Whigs, not from any affinity with those of the Revolution, but because the name had a savour of liberty, and thus formed a convenient cover for those whose interests led to the support of slavery. Boston became one of the localities where the head-quarters of the Whigs was established, and of course became identified with the cotton-spinning and cotton-weaving interests. Here, therefore, the interests of the slaveholder were espoused with zeal, under the guise of upholding the constitution of the United States, of which the provision for returning runaway slaves began to appear a most important feature.'

And so, by general confession, the protracted and seemingly high-souled contest to check the progress of slavery, has been only a disguise under which to advance the interests of party. We are, in fact, to understand, that until the present time, the great thing held in view, is the power of returning members to congress to suit particular purposes, and that an objection to slavery has never attained the position of a substantive question—scarcely been ever anything else than a convenient sham. On the seizure of Texas, and afterwards on the outbreak of the war with Mexico—whenever fresh territory for slavery purposes was to be added to the Union—the Whigs blazed forth 'Resolutions,' about 'the duty of the free states not to submit.' But with the firing off of these wind-guns, 'the clamour, the courage, and patriotism of the Whigs oozed away;' and on each occasion, when the special object for noisy demonstration was one way or other set at rest—as has been recently exhibited in the case of Kansas—down sunk all ebullition of public, or more properly, party sentiment. Are the modern republicans to be more sincere and trustworthy than the now 'fossilised' Whigs? We know not. Avowing a merely defensive policy, they have disclaimed any intention to interfere with southern institutions; and looking at the past, we may be pardoned for not entertaining high expectations of what is to ensue should they get into power—an event in itself doubtful. Meanwhile, strong language is occasionally used by 'free-soilers' in and out of congress, denunciatory of slaveholders, and we always seem to be on the eve of something being done to put an end to slavery. Alas! after talking and scheming for the last fifty years, slavery is more vigorous and lifelike than ever. According to the well-known ratio of increase—about 150,000 per annum—the present number of slaves in the United States cannot be fewer than 4,100,000, shewing an addition of 900,000 since 1850. We think it may be safely averred that party manœuvring has had a fair trial and been found wanting. Slavery is to be abated neither by abuse, nor by selfish political partisanship. The free states, if they feel inclined, may appoint representatives in congress who could shiver the principle of squatter sovereignty to atoms, and consequently reduce slavery to a sectional institution, preliminary to its extinction. How, in the aggregate, they have failed to do so, let late elections testify.

In the spring and summer of 1856, the illegal proceedings of the Missourians in Kansas, produced much resentment throughout the free states—discussions on the subject being, doubtless, aggravated with a covert reference to the approaching presidential election. In congress, too, the struggle in Kansas produced a debate, whence arose an incident which takes a prominent place in the history of American slavery. We allude to that most dastardly and disgraceful assault on the person of Mr Sumner, which no provocation could justify.

The Hon. Charles Sumner, for some years a member of senate from Massachusetts, and a lawyer by profession, is at present one of the most accomplished scholars and orators in the United States—as a freesoiler, an uncompromising enemy of slavery, and well known for his advocacy of all proper measures for social melioration. If we were asked to name a member of the supreme legislature, of whom the American people had reason to be specially proud, we would unhesitatingly refer to Charles Sumner. Mild and gentlemanly in manners, he is the last person whom we could have supposed to be the victim of the unseemly outrage, of which we may give a brief account. On the 19th and 20th of May 1856, Mr Sumner delivered in his place in the senate at Washington, one of his most effective harangues on the iniquities which had been perpetrated in Kansas. Calling on the legislature for redress, he began by describing the crime which had been promoted by the Slave Power—an oligarchy exercising a thraldom which it was his intention and duty to expose. He then proceeded:

'Before entering upon the argument, I must say something of a general character, particularly in response to what has fallen from senators who have raised themselves to eminence on this floor in championship of human wrongs; I mean the senator from South Carolina [A. P. Butler], and the senator from Illinois [S. A. Douglas], who, though unlike as Don Quixote and Sancho Panza, yet, like this couple, sally forth together in the same adventure. I regret much to miss the elder senator from his seat; but the cause, against which he has run a tilt, with such activity of animosity, demands that the opportunity of exposing him should not be lost; and it is for the cause that I speak. The senator from South Carolina has read many books of chivalry, and believes himself a chivalrous knight, with sentiments of honour and courage. Of course he has chosen a mistress, to whom he has made his vows, and who, though ugly to others, is always lovely to him; though polluted in the sight of the world, is chaste in his sight—I mean the harlot, Slavery. For her, his tongue is always profuse in words. Let her be impeached in character, or any proposition made to shut her out from the extension of her wantonness, and no extravagance of manner or hardihood of assertion is then too great for this senator. The frenzy of Don Quixote, in behalf of Dulcinea del Toboso, is all surpassed. The asserted rights of slavery, which shock equality of all kinds, are cloaked by a fantastic claim of equality. If the slave states cannot enjoy what, in mockery of the great fathers of the republic, he misnames equality under the constitution—in other words, the full power in the national territories to compel fellow-men to unpaid toil, to separate husband and wife, and to sell little children at the auction-block—then, sir, the chivalric senator will conduct the state of South Carolina out of the Union! Heroic knight! Exalted senator! A second Moses come for a second exodus!

'But not content with this poor menace, which we have been twice told was "measured," the senator, in the unrestrained chivalry of his nature, has undertaken to apply opprobrious words to those who differ from him on this floor. He calls them "sectional and fanatical;" and opposition to the usurpation in Kansas, he denounces as "an uncalculating fanaticism." To be sure, these charges lack all grace of originality, and all sentiment of truth; but the adventurous senator does not hesitate. He is the uncompromising, unblushing representative on this floor of a flagrant *sectionalism*, which now domineers over the republic; and yet with a ludicrous ignorance of his own position —unable to see himself as others see him—or with an effrontery which even his white head ought not to protect from rebuke, he applies to those here who resist his *sectionalism* the very epithet which designates himself. The men who strive to bring back the government to its original policy, when freedom and not slavery was national, while slavery and not freedom was sectional, he arraigns as *sectional*. This will not do. It involves too great a perversion of terms. I tell that senator, that it is to himself, and to the "organisation" of which he is the "committed advocate," that this epithet belongs. I now fasten it upon them. For myself, I care little for names; but since the question has been raised here, I affirm that the republican party of the Union is in no just sense *sectional*, but, more than any other party, *national;* and that it now goes forth to dislodge from the high places of the government, the tyrannical sectionalism of which the senator from South Carolina is one of the maddest zealots.

'To the charge of fanaticism I also reply: Sir, fanaticism is found in an enthusiasm or exaggeration of opinions, particularly on religious subjects; but there may be a fanaticism for evil as well as for good. Now, I will not deny that there are persons among us loving liberty too well for their personal good, in a selfish generation. Such there may be, and, for the sake of their example, would that there were more! In calling them "fanatics," you cast contumely upon the noble army of martyrs, from the earliest day down to this hour; upon the great tribunes of human rights, by whom life, liberty, and happiness, on earth, have been secured; upon the long line of devoted patriots, who, throughout history, have truly loved their country; and, upon all, who, in noble aspirations for the general good, and in forgetfulness of self, have stood out before their age, and gathered into their generous bosoms the shafts of tyranny and wrong, in order to make a pathway for truth. You discredit Luther, when alone he nailed his articles to the door of the church at Wittenberg, and then, to the imperial demand that he should retract, firmly replied: "Here I stand; I cannot do otherwise, so help me God!" You discredit Hampden, when alone he refused to pay the few shillings of ship-money, and shook the throne of Charles I.; you discredit Milton, when, amidst the corruptions of a heartless court, he lived on, the lofty friend of liberty, above question of suspicion; you discredit Russell and Sidney, when, for the sake of their country, they calmly turned from family and friends, to tread the narrow steps of the scaffold; you discredit those early founders of American institutions, who preferred the hardships of a wilderness, surrounded

by a savage foe, to injustice on beds of ease; you
discredit our later fathers, who, few in numbers and
weak in resources, yet strong in their cause, did not
hesitate to brave the mighty power of England, already
encircling the globe with her morning drum-beats.
Yes, sir, of such are the fanatics of history, according
to the senator. But I tell that senator, that there are
characters badly eminent, of whose fanaticism there can
be no question. Such were the ancient Egyptians, who
worshipped divinities in brutish forms; the Druids,
who darkened the forests of oak, in which they lived,
by sacrifices of blood; the Mexicans, who surrendered
countless victims to the propitiation of their obscene
idols; the Spaniards, who, under Alva, sought to force
the Inquisition upon Holland, by a tyranny kindred to
that now employed to force slavery upon Kansas; and
such were the Algerines, when in solemn conclave, after
listening to a speech not unlike that of the senator
from South Carolina, they resolved to continue the
slavery of white Christians, and to extend it to the
countrymen of Washington! Ay, sir, extend it! And
in this same dreary catalogue faithful history must
record all who now, in an enlightened age, and in a land
of boasted freedom, stand up, in perversion of the
constitution, and in denial of immortal truth, to fasten
a new shackle upon their fellow-man. If the senator
wishes to see fanatics, let him look round among his
own associates; let him look at himself.

'But I have not done with the senator. There is
another matter regarded by him of such consequence,
that he interpolated it into the speech of the senator
from New Hampshire [J. P. Hale], and also announced
that he had prepared himself with it, to take in his
pocket all the way to Boston, when he expected to
address the people of that community. On this account,
and for the sake of truth, I stop for one moment, and

tread it to the earth. The North, according to the senator, was engaged in the slave-trade, and helped to introduce slaves into the southern states; and this undeniable fact he proposed to establish by statistics, in stating which his errors surpassed his sentences in number. But I let these pass for the present, that I may deal with his argument. Pray, sir, is the acknowledged turpitude of a departed generation to become an example for us? And yet the suggestion of the senator, if entitled to any consideration in this discussion, must have this extent. I join my friend from New Hampshire in thanking the senator from South Carolina for adducing this instance; for it gives me an opportunity to say, that the northern merchants, with homes in Boston, Bristol, Newport, New York, and Philadelphia, who catered for slavery during the years of the slave-trade, are the lineal progenitors of the northern men, with homes in these places, who lend themselves to slavery in our day; and especially that all, whether north or south, who take part, directly or indirectly, in the conspiracy against Kansas, do but continue the work of the slave-traders, which you condemn. It is true, too true, alas! that our fathers were engaged in this traffic; but that is no apology for it. And in repelling the authority of this example, I repel also the trite argument founded on the earlier example of England. It is true that our mother-country, at the peace of Utrecht, extorted from Spain the Assiento Contract, securing the monopoly of the slave-trade with the Spanish colonies, as the whole price of all the blood of great victories; that she higgled at Aix-la-Chapelle for another lease of this exclusive traffic; and again, at the treaty of Madrid, clung to the wretched piracy. It is true, that in this spirit the power of the mother-country was prostituted to the same base ends in her American colonies, against indignant protests from our fathers. All these things now rise up in judgment against her. Let us not follow the senator from South Carolina to do the very evil to-day, which in another generation we condemn.'

Next, referring to Mr Douglas, senator from Illinois, he proceeded: 'Standing on this floor, the senator issued his rescript, requiring submission to the usurped power of Kansas; and this was accompanied by a manner—all his own—such as befits the tyrannical threat. Very well. Let the senator try. I tell him now that he cannot enforce any such submission. The senator, with the slave-power at his back, is strong, but he is not strong enough for this purpose. He is bold. He shrinks from nothing. Like Danton, he may cry, "*L'audace! l'audace! toujours l'audace!*" but even his audacity cannot compass this work. The senator copies the British officer, who, with boastful swagger, said that with the hilt of his sword he would cram the "stamps" down the throats of the American people; and he will meet a similar failure. He may convulse this country with civil feud. Like the ancient madman, he may set fire to this temple of constitutional liberty, grander than Ephesian dome; but he cannot enforce obedience to that tyrannical usurpation.

'The senator dreams that he can subdue the North. He disclaims the open threat, but his conduct still implies it. How little that senator knows himself, or the strength of the cause which he persecutes! He is but a mortal man; against him is an immortal principle. With finite power, he wrestles with the infinite, and he must fall. Against him are stronger battalions than any marshalled by mortal arm—the inborn, ineradicable, invincible sentiments of the human heart; against him is nature in all her subtle forces; against him is God. Let him try to subdue these.'

We need not follow Mr Sumner through his lengthened speech, for the narrative of the struggle in Kansas, which formed its main feature, has been already presented in these pages. In concluding, he admonitorily appealed to the sense of justice of the people. 'The contest which, beginning in Kansas, has reached us, will soon be transferred from congress to a broader stage, where every citizen will be not only spectator, but actor; and to their judgment I confidently appeal. To the people, now on the eve of exercising the electoral franchise, in choosing a chief magistrate of the republic, I appeal, to vindicate the electoral franchise in Kansas. Let the ballot-box of the Union, with multitudinous might, protect the ballot-box in that territory. Let the voters everywhere, while rejoicing in their own rights, help to guard the equal rights of distant fellow-citizens; that the shrines of popular institutions, now desecrated, may be sanctified anew; that the ballot-box, now plundered, may be restored; and that the cry, "I am an American citizen," may not be sent forth in vain against outrage of every kind. In just regard for free labour in that territory, which it is sought to blast by unwelcome association with slave labour; in Christian sympathy with the slave, whom it is proposed to task and to sell there; in stern condemnation of the crime which has been consummated on that beautiful soil; in rescue of fellow-citizens, now subjugated to a tyrannical usurpation; in dutiful respect for the early fathers, whose aspirations are now ignobly thwarted; in the name of the constitution, which has been outraged—of the laws trampled down—of justice banished—of humanity degraded—of peace destroyed—of freedom crushed to earth; and, in the name of the Heavenly Father, whose service is perfect freedom, I make this last appeal.'

Candidly considered, there were some passages in this speech neither in the best taste, nor in accordance with English notions of parliamentary licence; but there was nothing out of the usual routine of congressional harangues on occasions of party difference; and we have to remember that Mr Sumner spoke under a deep sense of the grievous wrongs committed in Kansas, through the agency of the party of which Mr Butler and Mr Douglas were, in a sense, the leaders. Whatever may be thought of Mr Sumner's harangue, nothing could justify the form of reprisal, a bare allusion to which shocks every sensitive feeling.

Mr Sumner's speech enraged the extreme southern party in congress; and as is now alleged, the Hon. Preston S. Brooks,* member of the House of Representatives, from South Carolina, was appointed to commit an assault on Mr Sumner, under the name of a chastisement for his allusions to Mr Butler, who was at the time absent. Whether Brooks so acted from the incitement of his friends or only from his own will, is indifferent. On the 22d of May, the senate adjourned at an early hour, in consequence of the death of a member; but after the adjournment, as is not unusual with senators, Mr Sumner remained at his desk writing. There were also present Mr Crittenden, of Kentucky, and several other senators, who had not left the chamber, some of the subordinate officers, and a number of other persons. While Mr Sumner was seated writing, Mr Brooks, accompanied by Mr Keitt,

---

* Members of both branches of congress receive the title of Honourable, which they seem to retain through life — a curious example of titular distinction in a republican country.

from the same state, entered, and forthwith Brooks with a cane struck Mr Sumner a severe blow over the head. Mr Sumner sprang from his seat, but staggered under the effect of the blow, reeling about and falling partially over the desk. Notwithstanding his helpless condition, Brooks repeated his blows with great force and rapidity. Mr Sumner, who lay on the floor in a state of partial stupor, was raised by his friends, and carried into the outer apartment, where medical service was promptly procured. No one of the many persons about, interfered to check the outrage, the explanation of this somewhat strange circumstance being that the attack was sudden and unexpected.

Such is the substance of the reports given of this horrible affair in the New York and Boston newspapers. The following is the statement of Mr Sumner:

'I attended the senate as usual on Thursday, the 22d of May. After some formal business, a message was received from the House of Representatives, announcing the death of a member of that body from Missouri. This was followed by a brief tribute to the deceased from Mr Geyer, of Missouri, when, according to usage and out of respect to the deceased, the senate adjourned at once. Instead of leaving the senate-chamber with the rest of the senators, on the adjournment, I continued in my seat, occupied with my pen, and while thus intent, in order to be in season for the mail, which was soon to close, I was approached by several persons who desired to converse with me, but I answered them promptly and briefly, excusing myself for the reason that I was much engaged. When the last of these persons left me, I drew my arm-chair close to my desk, and with my legs under the desk continued writing. My attention at this time was so entirely drawn from all other subjects that, though there must have been many persons in the senate, I saw nobody. While thus intent, with my head bent over my writing, I was addressed by a person who approached the front of my desk; I was so entirely absorbed that I was not aware of his presence until I heard my name pronounced. As I looked up with pen in hand, I saw a tall man, whose countenance was not familiar, standing directly over me, and at the same moment caught these words: "I have read your speech twice over carefully; it is a libel on South Carolina, and Mr Butler, who is a relative of mine." While these words were still passing from his lips, he commenced a succession of blows with a heavy cane on my bare head, by the first of which I was stunned so as to lose my sight. I saw no longer my assailant, nor any other person or object in the room. What I did afterward was done almost unconsciously, acting under the instincts of self-defence. With head already bent down, I rose from my seat—wrenching up my desk, which was screwed to the floor—and then pressing forward, while my assailant continued his blows. I had no other consciousness until I found myself ten feet forward in front of my desk, lying on the floor of the senate, with my bleeding head supported on the knee of a gentleman whom I soon recognised by voice and manner as Mr Morgan, of New York. Other persons there were about me offering me friendly assistance, but I did not recognise any of them. Others there were at a distance, looking on and offering no assistance, of whom I recognised only Mr Douglas, of Illinois, Mr Toombs, of Georgia, and I thought also my assailant standing between them. I was helped from the floor and conducted into the lobby of the senate, where I was placed upon a sofa. Of those who helped me here, I have no recollection. As I entered the lobby, I recognised Mr Slidell, of Louisiana, who retreated, but I recognised no one else until I felt a friendly grasp of the hand, which seemed to come from Mr Campbell, of Ohio. I have a vague impression that Mr Bright, president of the senate, spoke to me while I was on the floor of the senate or in the lobby. I make this statement in answer to the interrogatory of the committee, and offer it as presenting completely all my recollections of the assault and of the attending circumstances, whether immediately before or immediately after. I desire to add, that beside the words which I have given as uttered by my assailant, I have an indistinct recollection of the words "old man;" but these are so enveloped in the mist which ensued from the first blow, that I am not sure whether they were uttered or not.'

Mr Sumner's recovery was slow and doubtful, and till the present time, he has not been able to resume his senatorial duties. His appeal for legal redress was so poorly answered—damages being awarded to the amount of only 300 dollars—that faith in public justice, we should think, must be considerably shaken. The most extraordinary circumstance connected with the outrage, was the approval of Brooks's proceedings in the southern states. We may gather general opinion from the following tirade in the *Richmond Inquirer*, of June 12:

'In the main, the press of the South applaud the conduct of Mr Brooks, without condition or limitation. Our approbation, at least, is entire and unreserved. We consider the act good in conception, better in execution, and best of all in consequence. The vulgar abolitionists in the senate are getting above themselves. They have been humoured until they forget their position. They have grown saucy, and dare to be impudent to gentlemen! Now, they are a low, mean, scurvy set, with some little book-

learning, but as utterly devoid of spirit or honour as
a pack of curs. Intrenched behind "privilege," they
fancy they can slander the South, and insult its
representatives with impunity. The truth is, they
have been suffered to run too long without collars.
They must be lashed into submission. Sumner, in
particular, ought to have nine-and-thirty early every
morning. He is a great strapping fellow, and could
stand the cowhide beautifully. Brooks frightened
him, and at the first blow of the cane, he bellowed
like a bull-calf. In the absence of an adequate law,
southern gentlemen must protect their own honour
and feelings. It is an idle mockery to challenge one
of these scullions. It is equally useless to attempt
to disgrace them. They are insensible to shame, and
can be brought to reason only by an application of
cowhide or gutta-percha. Let them once understand
that for every vile word spoken against the South, they
will suffer so many stripes, and they will soon learn
to behave themselves like decent dogs—they can never
be gentlemen. Mr Brooks has initiated this salutary
discipline, and he deserves applause for the bold,
judicious manner in which he chastised the scamp
Sumner. It was a proper act, done at the proper
time, and in the proper place.

'Of all places on earth, the senate-chamber, the
theatre of his vituperative exploits, was the very spot
where Sumner should have been made to suffer for
his violation of the decencies of decorous debate, and
for his brutal denunciation of a venerable statesman.
It was literally and entirely proper that he should be
stricken down and beaten just beside the desk against
which he leaned as he fulminated his filthy utterances
through the capitol. It is idle to talk of the sanctity
of the senate-chamber, since it is polluted by the
presence of such fellows as Wilson, and Sumner, and

Wade. They have desecrated it, and cannot now fly to it as to a sanctuary from the lash of vengeance. We trust other gentlemen will follow the example of Mr Brooks, that so a curb may be imposed upon the truculence and audacity of abolition speakers. If need be, let us have a caning or cowhiding every day. If the worst come to the worst, so much the sooner, so much the better.'

The ovations to Brooks in South Carolina—the approval of his conduct at public meetings—the presenting him with elegantly mounted canes, and so forth, are vividly in the recollection of every reader. No event, take it from first to last, has been so derogatory to the American character in Europe; although, of course, it is allowed that blame should rest, where it has been indignantly put by the unanimous voice of the people of Massachusetts. We may know what that voice was, as well as learn a few useful particulars as to the relationship of North and South, from a speech delivered at Cambridge, near Boston, by Mr Richard Dana, junior, author of the popular work, *Two Years Before the Mast.* The following are the principal passages:

'The last census has demonstrated what many have declared, but few have believed, that under the form of a republic, this country is now, and has long been, governed by an oligarchy. In the free states there are now about 17,000,000 free inhabitants and no slaves. In the slave states there are 4,000,000 slaves, owned by 350,000 owners. These 350,000 owners of slaves own the valuable land and the labourers, and monopolise the government of the slave states. The non-slaveholding free population is of little account. This forms the privileged class, the oligarchy. It is not for the purpose of making them odious that I use this name. It is the only proper designation. Including the families of the owners, there may be 2,000,000 persons in the dominant class or order.

'This oligarchy has governed the whole country, and governs it now with a sway of increasing demands and exactions. Of seventeen presidential elections, natives of slave states have carried thirteen, and natives of free states four. Of the life of our government, forty-nine years have been passed under slaveholding chief magistrates, and eighteen under non-slaveholders. They have always had a majority of the judges of the supreme court of the United States. The population, the arts, the sciences, commerce, inventions, copyrights, manufactures, all are with the free states. Yet the slave states hold, and have always held the judiciary. They almost monopolised the army and navy when appointments were open. At this moment, though there are sixteen free states, and fifteen slave states, a majority of the senate are slaveholders. To make a long story short, there has never been a question between the slave power and the free power, on the floor of congress, in which the slave power has not triumphed.

'I will not go over the recital of the successive defeats of freedom and aggressions of slavery. The subjugation of Kansas is the latest triumph. The subjugation of free speech is its object now. At first, you recollect, no man can have forgotten, the right of petition was denied. For that John Quincy Adams perilled all a public man has to peril, and life itself. Next, through resolves of congress and platforms of both the great parties, they tried again to suppress free speech. Now, they chastise it by violence, in the very sanctuary of its refuge. No man has received a national nomination that is not acceptable to them. No man can be confirmed in a national office, from Secretary of State or minister at St James's to the humblest postmaster, that is not satisfactory to them. Mr Everett's appointment at St James's hung in suspense because he was suspected of having uttered, somewhere, a sentiment hostile to slavery and its interests. The country is one vast Dionysius's ear. Every whisper in the closet is transmitted and punished. Before parting to-night, let me ask any doubting friend, if there be one here, what provocation more he proposes to wait for? They have added slave states by a *coup d'état*; will you wait until they have added Cuba or Central America? They have tried to force slavery on Kansas; will you wait until they have succeeded? They have violated one solemn compact; how many more must they violate, before you will assert your right? They have struck down a senator in his place. Some of their presses have designated the next victim; will you wait until he has fallen?'

The assault by Mr Brooks did not escape reproof in the House of Representatives. He resigned, and was re-elected. Although his conduct so far met with the approval of his constituents, although fêted and lauded, Brooks was probably conscious that an indelible stain would rest on his reputation. At Washington, in the early part of the session 1856-7, he is said to have encountered cold looks from former acquaintances. His fate was remarkable. He was suddenly seized with an inflammation of the throat, resulting in croup. By this fatal disease, his life was abruptly and painfully terminated, January 27, 1857—an event which, from all the associated circumstances, could hardly fail to send a chill through that department of southern society which had indiscreetly applauded his outrage.

THE condition of slaves in the United States has been so luminously described in the recent works of Mrs Stowe and others, that further explanations do not seem to be necessary. It is now pretty well known, that, by the laws of the southern states, a slave, whatever be his colour, belongs as a piece of movable property to his master, who may sell him, put him to any kind of labour he deems advisable, appropriate his earnings, and feed, clothe, and retain him in an abject servitude till the end of his days. Like one of the lower animals, a slave is a 'chattel personal,' a thing without rights; his duty being unqualified submission to the will of his proprietor. To carry out the comparison with the lower animals, the slave cannot legally marry. He may indeed go through the ceremonial of marriage, but the tie is altogether invalid. As regards progeny, the law is, that children follow the condition of the mother; children born in slavery, therefore, are the property of the owner. A slave can raise no suit at law on claim of damage or assault. If injured by a third party, his master may alone sue for damages, in the same manner as if he complained of an injury done to his horse. The master may punish his slave without mercy; whip, cudgel, brand, and torture him as he thinks fit. Though owners may not lawfully and wilfully put their slaves to death, practically, according to all accounts, they occasionally do so, through the impulse of passion, to the sacrifice of their property. At all events, whatever cruelties are perpetrated on a southern estate, no slave can bear witness against them, for legally he is not permitted to make a declaration on oath against whites. Worthless, unfriended, it appears to be still a question in law whether he is a reasonable being.

The natural increase of slaves on a plantation causes a continual pressure on the means of owners. More are born than are wanted for local purposes, and the overplus, as a matter of necessity, must be sold to traders for transfer to public markets; and on such occasions there occur most distressing separations among members of families. There is, however, reason to believe, that in many instances, planters part with their servants with reluctance, and only under the pressure of extreme necessity. We do not mention the fact from our own knowledge, but from what we heard stated in America, that in some cases, masters are relieved of an embarrassment, by slaves asking to be sold; the slaves in such cases being influenced by the false representations of decoy-negroes sent to recruit for labourers. That there frequently exists the most kindly feeling between the families of proprietors and their slave dependents, is undeniable; and it is the spectacle of this harmony between master and servant, that fascinates travellers in the South, and induces them to declare that slavery is by no means so bad a thing as it is usually represented.

Unhappily, the slave has no security in the indulgence of his proprietor. He is at all times liable to be sold on account of the death, insolvency, not to speak of the ordinary necessities, of his owner; and may at any moment be precipitated from a state of comparative comfort to a condition of utter wretchedness. Some owners, affected by the evils of slavery, would, though at a great pecuniary sacrifice, emancipate their slaves, and so leave them to assume the status of free labourers. But, independently of a general dislike of free labour in the South, there are laws to check the benevolent intentions of slave-owners. Emancipations take place in particular circumstances, and by tolerance in certain states; but as a general rule, an owner desiring to liberate his slaves would need to send them into the free states or out of the country. Were he to emancipate them in defiance of this law, without exiling them, they would be seized and sold by the public authorities; by which arrangement liberation is, to a great extent, impracticable. These difficulties, however, cannot be deemed an apology for slavery. If owners were generally disposed to adopt means for securing freedom to their slaves, they could surely agitate for a reconsideration of the state laws which at present hamper their operations. According to southern notions, the freeing of slaves is immoral—a crime against social order. The slaves, consequently, are not allowed to purchase their own freedom, by the savings of extra industry. The whole earnings of a slave belong to his master; unless by particular favour, he can retain nothing for himself. In Brazil, as was the law in the British West Indies, slaves are humanely entitled to certain holidays, which are at their own disposal, by which arrangement they are enabled to cultivate small patches of land, and accumulate wherewith to buy their freedom. In the United States, the slaves can legally claim no holidays; though a week at Christmas is usually granted, and in most quarters they are allowed to be at rest on Sunday. This denial of the power of labouring to buy themselves from their owners, forms a feature in American slavery which distinguishes it from aught in ancient or modern times. The slavery of Russia is liberty itself, in comparison. A natural result is the desire to escape, in defiance of all precautions to the contrary. Large numbers flee from slavery, and through the aid of friends at different parts of the country, make their way to Western Canada. One person with whom we have been made acquainted, has afforded means of escape to upwards of 2000 slaves, and we doubt not he will, from a conscientious feeling of duty, help away many more. So numerous are now the channels of escape, that towards the more northern sections of the slave states, owners begin to entertain a sense of considerable insecurity in their human property.

Besides fears on this account, slave-owners over the whole South are less or more under a constant apprehension of outbreak; the best evidence of their uneasiness being the rigorous measures of coercion by which their power is sustained. As a security against plots for insurrection or escape, the slave in the United States is necessarily kept in ignorance. It is illegal to teach him to read; and although some masters and mistresses evade the law in this respect, the slaves generally know nothing of the arts of reading and writing. Further, they are not allowed to travel from home without written passes, which, in their ignorance of letters, they are unable to counterfeit. The seizure and imprisonment of vagrant slaves form a staple subject of advertisements in southern newspapers; and so likewise is the tracking of runaways by means of 'negro dogs' a matter of frequent announcement.

Such is an outline of the ordinary condition of American slaves—in some states better, and in other states worse, according to circumstances. An anticipated insurrection, for example, being always followed with additional severities; such as, preventing the slaves from assembling for religious worship, or from enjoying various petty indulgences. Among the fifteen slave states, that of Delaware possesses the most liberal slave code; and but for party manœuvring, a small exertion would add it to the number of the free states. In travelling southward, the stranger becomes aware that he has passed the boundary of freedom, by the general aspect of dilapidation in the rural districts, by the want of commercial life in the towns, and in particular, by the appearance, for the first time, of soldiers on guard in the evenings at public buildings—a phenomenon strikingly indicative of a peculiar and not very satisfactory social condition.

Despite the various restrictions on emancipation and the settlement of free negroes, there have grown up throughout the slave states a certain number of free persons of colour—some black, others nearly as light in the complexion as whites. In Louisiana, in particular, free persons of colour own large possessions, though labouring under social disabilities. The number of free coloured persons in the whole of the slave states, in 1850, amounted to 228,128. In the free states, at the same period, there were 196,016 free persons of colour; the total number in the Union being 424,144.

From all that fell under my observation in America, I arrived at the conviction that as long as the free persons of colour were legally and socially oppressed in the northern states, the people of these states generally could not with a good grace address remonstrances to the South on the subject of slavery; and, indeed, an entire reversal of free-state policy on this point, would, in my opinion, be necessary as a preliminary to making any proposal to southern planters that they should dismiss their slaves and resort to free labour. It is not possible to speak without indignation of the contumelies to which free coloured persons are exposed throughout the United States; and what is most offensive of all is, that more flagrant cases of maltreatment occur in the North than the South—affectedly religious people in various free states shrinking with much greater horror from coloured individuals in railway-cars and hotels than even 'southern chivalry.' Yet, the laws respecting free persons of colour in most of the slave states are sufficiently barbarous, and any relaxations in the way of personal intercourse depend more on private than public feeling.

In the southern states, free persons of colour have always been a source of anxiety, in consequence of the increase in their numbers and their advancement in wealth and intelligence. Their very success as free labourers and artisans is viewed ungraciously, for it is a standing protest against the often-repeated doctrine, that if the slaves were emancipated they would not work, and so become a dangerous class and a burden to the community. As conservative of slavery, it has been deemed desirable to repress the rise of free coloured persons to situations of trust, by the enactment of numerous disqualifying laws. In Virginia, these laws are exceedingly obnoxious. In this state, it is a penal offence to teach free coloured children to read—imprisonment to a white person, and stripes or imprisonment to a negro. Two or three years ago, a lady was imprisoned for this offence. In Virginia, a free negro cannot keep a gun in his house, under a penalty of stripes or imprisonment. He must not go from home after dark, unless provided with a pass; annual licences or passes are issued for a certain fee. He must not keep a store or tavern; every effort being made to restrict him to such industrial pursuits as will not compete with the white business part of the community. Should he leave the state, and go even for the shortest distance into a free state, he returns only at the risk of being imprisoned and tried for the offence; if found guilty, he is ordered to leave the state within ten days, never to return, except under the penalty of being sold as a slave. He may hold real estate in his own name, a rather remarkable indulgence; but in the condition of an owner of property, and in his attempts to conduct any business transaction, he is greatly hampered in consequence of his testimony not being valid in a court of justice, in any case where the interests of a white man are at stake, or where his evidence would conflict with that of one of the governing class. The taxes that Virginia imposes on this unfortunate class are burdensome in the extreme. In addition to the numberless petty rates they are compelled to pay to city and county authorities, a state tax of one dollar per head has been levied from them for the last five years; from which the state annually derives a revenue of nearly, if not quite, fifty thousand dollars. The tax was originally imposed as an aid towards removing free persons of colour to Liberia, but has latterly been misappropriated.

As a general rule in slave states, every free person of colour is obliged to procure from the court of the county in which he resides, a set of papers to shew when required, in proof of his freedom. Should he quit the state, he will find that even these papers, which any white man may demand a sight of, are not considered sufficient evidences of freedom, without additional sworn testimony of some well-known white citizen. Should he, when in a distant part of the country, by any misfortune lose his 'free papers,' as they are called, he is at any moment liable to arrest; his colour being presumptive evidence that he is a fugitive slave. If arrested, and unable to communicate with his friends, he would be detained in jail for a certain period, be advertised, and if unable to pay prison and other expenses, he would be sold by public auction, like a stray heifer.

Free coloured persons with more than three quarters of white blood, are relieved from the operation of the laws which bear with most severity on those of darker complexion. They may engage in any business that the extent of their capital will admit; their testimony will be received in court in opposition to that of white citizens; and they may leave the state and return at pleasure. But by these concessions, they gain no social status; nor do they acquire political equality with whites. Free coloured persons of any shade are pronounced by federal authority not to be citizens under the constitution—a fact formerly adverted to, in speaking of a recent case.

In North Carolina, the laws affecting coloured persons are as severe as they are in Virginia, if not more so. According to one of these laws, a free coloured person incurs a penalty of 500 dollars on entering and residing in the state, and failing payment, he will be sold as a slave for a sufficient length of time to pay the amount. Lately, a young man, a free coloured seaman, from the state of New York, having shipped to a port in North Carolina, he was there detained by illness, and shortly afterwards put in jail. Some parties on the spot interested themselves in him, and with immense trouble, he was released. His journey homewards, in company of a white person, was attended with extreme difficulty. The account of the whole transaction occupies three columns in the *Tribune*, New York newspaper, February 13, 1857, and gives a vivid idea of the troubles and perils to which free coloured persons from the North expose themselves within the verge of the slave states.

In South Carolina, free coloured children enjoy a remarkable immunity; they are permitted to go to school. In Charleston, the principal city of the state, there is an excellent school supported entirely by the free coloured people, who form an intelligent and industrious body. They are, however, exposed to many annoyances, and made to feel their subordinate condition. A free coloured man must not carry a cane, and his wife is not allowed to wear a veil. Should they walk out together in the street, she must not take his arm; that would be regarded as an act of flagrant impertinence. If they meet a white person, and the path is narrow, they must go aside into the gutter to give unobstructed passage to a white. Even in their dwellings, they are not safe from indignities. The sound of many voices issuing at night from their houses is a suspicious circumstance, and will warrant the intrusion of any white person to inquire the cause.

When a coloured mother wishes to have her infant christened, and desires to invite a few friends to be present, she must inquire at her white neighbours if they have any objections to the proposed party; then, she must procure the permission of the authorities, without which the whole assembly might be arrested, punished with fine or stripes, at the option of the magistrate. In this, as in other slave states, all mechanical pursuits are open to free coloured persons, for, as it is deemed a degradation to a white man to engage in manual labour, no competition is feared. But they are not allowed to enter the learned professions, nor can they in any slave state, except Louisiana, where there are a few coloured physicians and some men of colour engaged in commercial pursuits.

In Georgia, in addition to the usual disabilities, a free coloured person is not permitted to hold real estate in his own name. He is compelled, no matter what be his age, to select a white guardian, who holds his property, and is answerable for him in law. Should the guardian prove faithless to his trust, his ward has no redress, as no evidence of his would have a feather's weight when opposed to that of a white.

In Louisiana, as above stated, the free coloured people are more privileged—a circumstance perhaps traceable to the kindliness of the French towards the negro race. From whatever cause, the oath of a coloured man in a court of justice has equal weight with that of a white citizen. Several attempts have been made to extinguish this privilege, and render the laws of the state more in harmony with those of other slave states; but on the side of negro testimony are arrayed strong interests, some of the largest land claims in the state being sustained by the testimony of persons belonging to this class. The very great mixture of races in Louisiana probably assists in thus doing something like justice. For years, the free coloured people of New Orleans were taxed to support the public schools of the city, and at the same time no provision was made for the education of their own children. For some time, the public school committee refused any appropriation to support schools for free coloured children, nor were these children allowed to attend the schools for whites. At length, after receiving numerous petitions, the committee was induced to make an appropriation of a very limited kind, which was gratefully accepted, though very inadequate to meet the general wants.

The laws of Texas, Alabama, Tennessee, and Missouri are in their general character like those of Virginia. In Texas there are severe laws against introducing free people of colour, enacted with additional penalties in 1856; yet, we are told by Olmsted that many of this class, from Louisiana, have established themselves in the state, though at the cost of feuds and bloodshed. The laws of Kentucky are somewhat milder; but there, as elsewhere, much depends on transitory circumstances

—law and administration, in slave states especially, being two very diffcrent things.

The insurrections that have occurred at various times in different parts of the South, have invariably been disastrous to the free people of colour, though they have been no way concerned in the negro outbreaks. The contemplated insurrection of Denmark Vesey in South Carolina, which was discovered only a short time before the period appointed for the outbreak, deprived the free coloured people of many privileges which they had enjoyed. A subsequent attempt of a similar character in Virginia, under the leadership of Nat Turner, was followed by corresponding results. The recent real or alleged attempt at insurrection in Tennessee, bids fair to entail more severe suffering on the free coloured population than any previous transaction of this nature. A law has been lately under consideration in Arkansas, which, if carried, will in all probability consign at least an eighth part of the now free coloured population to slavery. By the provisions of this bill, the alternative is presented to the free coloured people in the state, either immediate removal, or unconditional sale as slaves. Surrounded by slave states which forbid the ingress of free negroes, and with several hundred miles interposed between them and the free states, it can be imagined how little is the chance of escaping the penalties of this proposed law.

While in the slaveholding states, the free coloured people are subject to great injustice from the laws directly framed to oppress them, in the free states generally they have been persecuted by a cruel prejudice, that has not always allowed them to remain secure in life and limb. Their political and civil privileges differ in different states. The statute-books of Indiana and Illinois, both free states, are disgraced with a series of what are termed 'Black Laws;' the effect of which is to deprive the coloured man not only of all political privileges, but even the validity of his oath. The state of Ohio has repealed her black laws only within the last few years, after a long agitation on the subject. Yet, the laws respecting the qualification of voters are not clearly defined, and, as a consequence, in the northern part of the state, where a strong anti-slavery feeling prevails, free men of colour are permitted to vote; but in the southern districts that border on the slave state of Kentucky, the reverse is the rule. In Iowa, Michigan, Pennsylvania, and Connecticut, whilst they are not oppressed by direct legislation, they are deprived of all political privileges. In the state of New York, they are entitled to vote at elections, provided they are possessed of real estate to the value of 250 dollars. Gerrit Smith, a well-known philanthropist and reformer, about six years since, created in this state nearly one thousand voters in this class, by endowing them with property for the necessary qualification from his vast landed possessions. In all the New-England States, Connecticut excepted, the votes of free coloured persons are received on equal terms with those of the whites; and in Massachusetts, they are eligible to the highest offices in the gift of the commonwealth.

Nothing is more common in the northern states than to hear the free people of colour spoken of disparagingly, if not a nuisance which the country would be gladly rid of. As is well known, the plan of expatriation was proposed, and has been partly carried out by the American Colonisation Society, the well-conducted settlement of Liberia on the coast of Africa being the consequence. The remarkable prosperity of that free republic, which is susceptible of immense increase, indicates, if nothing else did, that the world has laboured under some mistake about the mental qualities of negroes and mulattoes; and, on this account, the plantation of Liberia, apart from all considerations as to the motives of its projectors, must, I think, be accepted as a great fact in favour of negro improvability. But it is not necessary to go to Liberia in vindication of the character of this abused branch of the human race. That the progenitors of the present free coloured population of northern states were degraded and ignorant, none will deny; but to say that their descendants, now in the third and fourth generation, are deserving of the same reputation, would be unjust and untruthful. Should we grant that they were generally degraded, which we by no means admit, can those who are inclined to disparage and revile them, point out what they have done towards their enlightenment and elevation? Far from assisting them on the road to honour and preferment, they have left no means untried to crush in them every noble aspiration, to forbid the rise of every sentiment of ambition, to keep the whole of every shade of darkness in a contemptuously mean position—exiles from all communion in joy, hope, sorrow.

The force and prevalence of this prejudice can scarcely be imagined by any one out of America. That the colour of a man's skin, without the slightest reference to his moral qualities, or to his wealth, should determine his social or political position, savours of the ridiculous to Europeans. Yet such is the case in the United States. Nay more, even when all trace of the negro is lost by intermixture, and he no longer presents any distinction in features, the knowledge that he has in some way come of African ancestry, is sufficient to place him in the proscribed list; he is consigned beyond the possibility of extrication to the difficult position sustained by the free coloured people of the northern states.

The sufferings endured by this class, from 1835 to 1842, were of a shocking kind. It was no unusual occurrence for an inoffensive man of colour, particularly if he was decently dressed, to be openly assaulted by white persons, for no cause whatever; and if his outcries attracted attention, no notice was taken when they were understood to come from 'only a nigger.' With the exception of a few abolitionists, the free coloured people had no friend; the agitation of the slave-question at that period being unscrupulously visited on them. In scarcely any of the large cities of the North did they escape violence. Riots of the most frightful nature occurred in New York, Philadelphia, Boston, and Cincinnati. The dwellings of the coloured people were burned down, their furniture destroyed, and their lives were taken by the miscreants who were permitted to give unchecked rein to their hateful passions. In some instances, their churches were razed to the ground, as if it had been a crime for this unfortunate race to form part of a Christian community.

This storm of persecution having passed over, the free coloured population in the northern states gradually improved in public opinion. In some quarters, and among certain classes of whites, prejudice is as strong as ever; but on the whole, it has been greatly meliorated—a circumstance attributable not less to the general progress of enlightened sentiment, than the feelings of compassion excited by the picturesque and affecting incidents in the lifelike narrations of Mrs Stowe. Yet, except in Massachusetts, these feelings do not go the length of giving complete justice to the people of colour. Though subject to a general school-rate, their children are not admitted to the higher kind of academies; the mere elements of education, at district coloured schools, being their full allowance.

In the Sabbath schools, the same division is observable. St Andrew's Episcopal Church at Philadelphia has under its patronage and care a black as well as a white Sabbath school, in separate establishments. Once in each year, the children of both schools are brought into the church, that their progress may be ascertained. The white lambs of the flock are placed beside the pastor under the shadow of the pulpit, whilst the black sheep are stuck up in an obscure part of the organ loft. The whites are usually catechised in presence of the congregation, and the blacks are kindly permitted to sing a doxology while the congregation are dispersing.

The common practice of excluding coloured people from all but certain inferior classes of seats in the churches, is well known; and to such an extent has this been carried, that in most large towns they have established and support churches for themselves. In passing along the streets of New York on Sunday, you see churches pouring out none but whites, and others none but people of various shades of colour, just as if there were a white and black Gospel. Only a few years ago, in one of the Presbyterian churches of New York, there were pews in the gallery marked B. M., signifying Black Members. An English clergyman on a visit to the States, who had heard of these proscribed seats, took an opportunity of testifying against such unchristian arrangements, by taking his family to this church, and seating himself in the midst of the B. M.s, to the astonishment and chagrin of the reverend gentleman who officiated, and the horror and disgust of the deacons, who were greatly scandalised by the stranger's want of self-respect. This quiet method of reproving the congregation of this church had the desired effect, and the B. M.s have since been removed. Negro pews are not now so fashionable as formerly; yet a coloured man would have to stand a long time in a genteel New York church before he would be offered a seat.

C. K. Whipple, in his able tract, entitled *Relations of Anti-slavery to Religion*, relates the following incident: 'In the year 1830, a coloured man bought and paid for a pew in Park Street Church, then and since the head-quarters of "orthodoxy" in Boston. He occupied it, with his family, a Sunday forenoon; but on returning in the afternoon, a constable, employed by the church committee, forcibly prevented his entrance; the Prudential Committee wrote him a prohibitory * letter; and the church, in a church-meeting called thereafter for the express purpose, *voted* that he should not be allowed to occupy his own pew. They then proceeded to discuss, in five or six meetings following, each opened and closed with prayer, the most convenient and effective way of excluding the whole coloured race from equal participation in their worship. Finally, at the suggestion of one who bore, while he lived, the very highest reputation for piety in that church, a new pew-deed was framed, containing a provision enabling them to effect their purpose, and the pews of that church are still held under that deed. It has been so perfectly obvious that any similar attempt would meet the like result, that the trial has never been repeated in Boston. A Baptist church, however (Rev. Baron Stow's, in Rowe Street), has guarded itself against such attempts, by inserting in its pew-deeds the restriction that the pews shall be sold only to "respectable

---

* 'BOSTON, *March* 6, 1830.

MR FREDERICK BRINSLEY.

SIR—The Prudential Committee of Park Street Church notify you not to occupy any pew on the lower floor of Park Street Meeting-house on any Sabbath, or on any other day during the time of divine worship, after this date; and if you go there with such intent, you hazard the consequences. The pews in the upper galleries are at your service.

GEORGE ODIORNE, *for the Committee*.'

white persons." Whoever of that congregation is not a saint, can at least claim the credit of being a respectable white sinner.'

Notwithstanding these and all other indignities, it is an undoubted fact, that the free people of colour persevere in improving their circumstances, and in seizing on every possible advantage in the way of education. Still excluded from the colleges in New York or Philadelphia, coloured young men are admitted as a favour to some of the other northern colleges and higher order of academies on a footing of equality with whites. The consequence of this irrepressible desire for instruction is observable in the rise of coloured men in northern society; there being now in Boston coloured lawyers practising at the bar, coloured physicians, lecturers, and manufacturers. A prejudice, however, long outlives its expulsion from the minds of the more intelligent classes, of which we have till this day a lamentable example in the treatment of Jews in England. Educated, refined in sentiment, wealthy, admitted to the highest society, Jews are still excluded by technical forms from the House of Commons; and time after time, the city of London returns a gentleman to parliament who is not allowed to take his seat, unless he make a declaration of a religious nature in violation of his conscience. So does prejudice operate in America. All are not to be blamed, because the free people of colour are subject to vulgar persecution. The prejudice against them has not yet vanished from the minds of every variety of the 'snob' genus. By white workmen, who fear rivalry and contamination; by conceited parvenus, who dread a lowering of their dignity; by a miscellaneous body of hotel-keepers, railway-car conductors, managers of theatres, deacons of churches, and others who are alarmed for offending 'customers,' the repugnance to associate with, or to give house or seat room to coloured people, is still daily manifested. Public feeling on the subject seems to be in a transition state. A coloured person, in travelling about, will sometimes be treated well, sometimes ill; sometimes insulted, sometimes passed over with indifference. The very administration of the law partakes of the feelings of its administrators.

Not long since, a coloured gentleman, a dealer in real estate, was compelled to ride in one of the negro-cars, although at the time he held stock in the company to the amount of ten thousand dollars. The ejection of a coloured lady and her infant from the cars in Massachusetts, created so much sympathy as to cause the passage of a law in that state, imposing a fine of six thousand dollars on any railway company or individual guilty of this offence in future. In the city of New York, suits have at various times been instituted against the proprietors of omnibuses and street railway-cars for the forcible ejection of coloured people. In one instance, judgment was given in favour of the plaintiff, and damages awarded to the amount of 250 dollars. But there is no dependence on these decisions. The case of the Rev. J. W. Pennington, a coloured preacher in New York, a most respectable and amiable person, who was well received in Europe, and holds a degree of Doctor of Divinity from the University of Heidelberg, deserves particular attention. Recently, he was expelled from a railway-car belonging to the Sixth Avenue Railway Company, and forthwith brought an action before the superior court of New York. Below, we give some notes of the proceedings in this curious affair, from the pages of the *European*, an independent New York newspaper.* It will be seen that the judge

---

* The counsel for the defendants contended that they were not bound to carry coloured people in all their cars. He referred to the constitution of

uttered some strange sentiments, and that the jury decided against Dr Pennington.

Mrs Webb, a coloured lady, apparently a quadroon, from the United States, has lately visited England on an elocutionary tour. Accomplished in manners, well educated, and every way acceptable as a guest in the houses of people of distinction, this lady has become well known for her elegant readings of the works of popular writers. It gives one a curious idea of American notions on colour, to know that this ladylike person has been subject to indignities in different

the United States, to shew that there was a line of demarcation between the two races, and asked the jury if a coloured man would be permitted to sit at the public table of the St Nicholas, or any of our principal hotels. He also stated that the number of cars provided by the defendants for the coloured people was larger in proportion to the population than the number for white people. Judge Slosson, in charging the jury, spoke of this as a peculiarly difficult case; the chief point for consideration being, whether the business and interests of the company would suffer, from allowing blacks an equality as passengers with whites. The jury, after two hours' deliberation, found a verdict for the defendants. The *European* quotes the following opinion from the New York *Herald:* 'Upon this point our northern people are remarkably squeamish, while we know that all over the South it is quite a common thing to see master and mistress and slave, whites and blacks, occupying the same stage or car, without any symptom of a turned-up nose on account of the presence of Pomp or Dinah.' The *European* adds the remark: 'If no legal distinctions were made in the free states between white and coloured men, the prejudice against the latter would soon disappear (it has no existence in Europe), and they would be allowed by the whites to work along with them, learn trades, and become lawyers and physicians. They are now a persecuted race—reviled, too, on account of the direct and inevitable consequences of the bad treatment to which they are subjected. When sick, they must be doctored, if at all, by a white physician; when their property, their lives, liberties, or reputations are imperilled by judicial procedures, if they have any counsel at all, he must be a white man—for no coloured man is, in this city, allowed to become a physician or a lawyer. It is different, however, in Massachusetts. This brutal prejudice, which exists in no other country, is encouraged by the slave-owners for their own purposes. The enforced degradation of the coloured man of the North is used as an argument for keeping up slavery in the South.'

parts of the states, for no other reason than she is not a pure white. She has mentioned to us, that in travelling through Pennsylvania, she was refused access to a railway-car, although she had purchased the appropriate ticket. On presenting herself for admission, the conductor put his arm across the door, to debar her entrance, and could not be induced to admit her. With much spirit, she stooped suddenly below his arm, and gaining an entrance, she pushed his arm down, to enable her husband to follow her into the car, where both received the congratulations of the passengers. The conductor was enraged, but, from the aspect of affairs, did not dare to expel them.

About a year ago, on visiting Boston, Mrs Webb went by recommendation to the Marlboro Hotel in that city. The Marlboro is known as 'the pious hotel.' It is an establishment celebrated for its religious usages—public prayers every morning, and a grace at every meal to which the guests assemble. Well, here, surely, she was safe? Quite the reverse. Mrs Webb was not allowed to attend prayers, nor to take her meals at the public tables, but compelled to remain in her own apartment. This was not all. The landlord had the meanness to charge the usual additional price for private meals, although remonstrated with, and shewn that exclusion from the public rooms was his own act. Much to the credit of the press of Massachusetts, this abominable treatment was strongly condemned; and we can fancy that by the drilling on the occasion, the Marlboro's sense of religious consistency must have undergone some improvement.

In Massachusetts and some other free states, coloured persons are legally recognised as American citizens; but this is only a local advantage. As formerly mentioned, the federal government does not allow that they belong to the category of citizens.

They are tolerated, and have a kind of protection; that is all. They will be given a pass, but not a passport. They are all of them 'niggers,' not Americans; and a few years ago it was no uncommon thing to hear an Irish or German immigrant, who had not been six months in the states, talk of sending the niggers out of the country, back to Africa, to which they belonged.

In the refusal of citizenship, the supreme government has forgotten the public services of the coloured race in the trying times of American history, when the clouds of adversity were most threatening. Answering to the call, blacks of every shade stood side by side with the whites in the revolutionary war. The first blood shed in the cause of American independence was that of Christopher Attocks, a mulatto, who was shot by British troops in the streets of Boston. In the swamps of the Carolinas, under the banners of Sumpter and Marion — with Lafayette at Yorktown, and with Washington at Valley Forge and Trenton—wherever the flag of the struggling Americans was unfurled, there might be found the negro cheerfully fighting for the national cause, for that liberty in which his descendants are denied to participate. Hundreds of coloured men, who are to-day deprived of all political privileges in the United States, can remember the scars displayed by their grandfathers—scars inflicted in defence of a country which has not only bestowed on their children obloquy and the hardest bondage, but denies their right to call themselves Americans.

To resume a former comparison, the free coloured people inhabiting the United States have, like the down-trodden Hebrew race in England and other parts of Europe, thriven under adversity. As the Jews, by being excluded from the enjoyment of common political privileges, bestowed their whole energies on certain branches of trade, and thus accumulated immense wealth, so have the free coloured race—negroes, mulattoes, quadroons, and so forth—betaken themselves to such industrial courses as were left open to them, and in many instances with the most favourable results. Though contemned or neglected, they form among themselves social circles of no mean quality. They dress as well as their white compeers; and in point of manners there is nothing, as a general rule, to find fault with. At all events, we can testify that the more aspiring among them who have visited Great Britain, do no discredit to the land of their nativity, and are treated in every respect as if they could boast of a purely Anglo-Saxon origin.

SLAVERY, and also the general prejudice against free people of colour, in the United States, are understood to have been in no small degree fortified by the conduct of the clergy of nearly every denomination—some better, some worse, but in too many instances, for the sake of conciliation, chargeable with perverting the religious doctrines which it is their duty to inculcate in a state of purity. It may be admitted that the position of clergymen, north as well as south, is exceedingly difficult and unpleasant. They see that the federal constitution and civil laws are in conflict with the law of the Gospel. Conviction may draw one way, livelihood another. Ministering to congregations who, to say the very least, are opposed to all action on the slavery question, it may be said their choice is in many quarters narrowed to the single point—either to follow public opinion, or give up preaching altogether, and so leave society in a state of spiritual destitution. Unfortunately, the American clergy do not confine themselves to passive obedience, nor with simply and conscientiously protesting on all suitable occasions against acts falling within the sphere of their duty. They industriously throw the weight of their influence and their dialectics on the side of slavery, which they make out to be a truly Christian institution, of the highest spiritual value to its victims; and, further, seize every opportunity of reviling those who advocate anti-slavery principles—calling them confusionists, infidels, and what not. Many clergymen in the South hold slaves; and also connive at their congregations possessing and hiring out slaves as a branch of ecclesiastical revenue. Clergy and congregations concur in occasionally raising funds for missionary schemes, Bible societies, and the erection of new places of worship by selling parcels of slaves. Joseph Sturge, in his *Visit to the United States* (1841), mentions the case of a congregation of Roman Catholics in Maryland, who sold some of their own church members in order to apply the proceeds to the building of a new place of public worship! How many of the clergy, likewise, at command, unite slaves in marriage, though quite aware that the ceremony is a mockery, and that the man and woman, perhaps both, are already married to other parties.* In short, instead of deploring this monstrous social evil, they absolutely encourage its growth, and speak of it as a marvellous blessing to the country. Who can speak with composure of this scandalous abuse of common sense and the most marked principles of Christianity? A grievous wrong is inflicted on the religion, of which these men pretend to be the true expositors.

Before us lie a number of documents containing flagrant evidences of this dereliction of duty; and in making a selection, the only difficulty is to know where to begin. We may at a venture first take up a pamphlet, purporting to be *Ten Letters on the Subject of Slavery*, by N. L. Rice, D.D., Pastor of the Second Presbyterian Church, St Louis, Missouri, published at

* 'At the Shiloh Baptist Association, which met at Gourdvine, a few years since, the following query, says the *Religious Herald*, was presented from Hedgman church—namely, Is a servant, whose husband or wife has been sold by his or her master, into a distant country, to be permitted to marry again? The query was referred to a committee, who made the following report, which, after discussion, was adopted: That, in view of the circumstances in which servants in this country are placed, the committee are unanimous in the opinion that it is better to permit servants thus circumstanced to take another husband or wife.'—*Key to Uncle Tom's Cabin*.

St Louis in 1855. Dr Rice writes to shew that those who oppose abolitionists do not fear discussion, and trusts that what he has to say will allay prejudice and passion. He considers slavery to be a providential fact, highly beneficial to the negro, and 'God has permitted it, for wise reasons, in order to the accomplishment of some great and important ends.' He then asks: 'Brethren, has it ever occurred to you, and to those with whom you act, that God has some great and benevolent ends to accomplish, by permitting slavery to exist in our country? You may regard this as a strange question; but although I have been in the habit, for years, of reading the writings of abolitionists, I do not remember to have seen the question discussed in a single instance. Their minds seem to have been fixed exclusively upon the wrongs which, as they suppose, have been inflicted upon the slaves; and their time and energies have been expended in condemning and denouncing slaveholders. The Presbyterian church has taken a widely different view. She has endeavoured to understand the designs of an All-wise Providence, in permitting the existence of slavery in our country. She has believed, that she did, to some extent, understand them; and her treatment of slavery has been influenced, in no small degree, by her views of the leadings of God's providence.'

In short, the African has been sent to America to 'receive the light of the Gospel;' and 'you will not deny, moreover, that the spiritual and eternal interests of the slaves are of infinitely greater importance than their freedom from human bondage.' In fact, abolition is a matter of 'comparatively trifling importance;' and 'you are compelled to admit that abolitionists, instead of rightly interpreting the providence of God, have perseveringly fought against it—that they have been the most determined enemies of a great work of God—one of the most important of this eventful age.' Slavery, Dr Rice afterwards says, was authorised by Moses, and no way denounced by the apostles. Abolitionism, by a natural consequence, leads to infidelity. 'No wonder, one of you told the General Assembly, last spring, of the unsettled state of men's minds in Massachusetts, and of the increase of infidelity there. If abolitionism much longer holds the sway, there will be little else there but infidelity.' Another argument—' Since the free states are throwing insuperable obstacles in the way of the settlement of free coloured people in their limits; and since the abolitionists denounce African colonisation, it really seems reasonable that they should stop their denunciations long enough to tell conscientious masters what to do with their slaves.' As for the churches in New England who may now denounce slavery, they never did so while slavery was sustained by law. 'Am I not correct? It passed away from New England rather because it was unprofitable, I presume, than because congregationalists expelled it. It required no extraordinary piety to denounce it, after it had passed away from you, and when you had nothing to lose by so doing.'

This slap at the New England clergy is perhaps not ill-deserved. The majority of them, we believe, made no objection to the Fugitive Slave Law; and it is stated on good authority, that many of them in sermons and otherwise openly approved of Webster's pro-slavery measures. In 1830, as formerly stated, a coloured family were excluded from their own purchased seat in Park Street Church, Boston. In May 1851, while Boston was agitated by the seizure of a refugee slave, the Rev. Dorus Clarke, minister of the Old South Church, refused to pray that God might be pleased to arouse the churches in that city to a sense of the duty of not delivering up this unhappy fugitive. On these and some other facts, Mr Whipple, in the tract already referred to, makes the following remarks:

'Park Street Church turns a coloured man, because he is coloured, out of a pew which he has bought and paid for, and then votes that no coloured man shall be allowed even to buy a pew any more among them; and their minister says nothing against it. Rowe Street Church votes that only respectable white persons shall own pews among them; and their minister says nothing against it. The minister of the Old South Church publicly defends slavery from the Bible, and his people agree with him. To carry out their idea of the best mode of promoting piety and good morals, they establish a daily meeting for prayer and exhortation. Whatever is "their hearts' sincere desire" in the departments of religion and good morals, it is appropriate to express in that meeting, to God by prayer, to men by exhortation. A man, who represents himself as a member of an evangelical church in communion with them, is kidnapped in their own city, and about to be enslaved for life in a region where the laws forbid him to read the Bible. His friend asks their prayers, exhortations, and efforts on his behalf. All these are refused, jointly refused by three persons, each a representative of the highest form of piety cultivated by that church and that meeting, and refused *because* piety is just then in an unusually flourishing state among them.'

As the anti-slavery cause grows in importance, we expect to hear that the New-England clergy will be able to assume a more independent position—will be able, one and all, to preach down the sentiment proclaimed by the Rev. Nehemiah Adams,* in his

* The vagaries of this and other 'evangelicals' produced the following Resolutions of the New England Anti-slavery Convention, May 1855: 'Whereas, the popular religion of the land is thoroughly impregnated with the slaveholding spirit, and from the organisation of the government to the present time has given its sanction to a colossal and ever-enlarging system of robbery, licentiousness, heathenism, and soul-murder, until the victims thereof are counted by millions; and whereas, an extensive revival of this religion is said to be going on in Boston, under the sanction and with the co-operation of such men as the Rev. Dr Nehemiah Adams and the Rev. Dr Blagden, the defenders of slavery against every assault upon it; therefore, resolved, That the multiplication of converts to such a religion, instead of indicating any progress in the cause of justice, freedom, and Christianity, or furnishing any occasion for congratulation, is a sure sign of moral degeneracy,

South-side View of Slavery, that 'While it [the constitution] remains, all our appeals to a Higher Law are fanaticism.'

J. G. Birney in a pamphlet, entitled *The American Churches the Bulwark of Slavery* (1840), cites some odious passages from the discourses of American clergymen, in favour of slavery. One of these says of slavery: 'It is not a moral evil. It is the Lord's doing, and marvellous in our eyes. And had it not done for the best, God alone, who is able, long since would have overruled it. It is by divine appointment.' We can fancy even southern men being disgusted with these sentiments.

Volumes could be filled with such extracts from sermons of American clergymen, not only vindicating slavery by the perversion of Scripture in its general scope and tendency, but misstating the meaning of the plainest texts. In the front rank of Bible-perverters stands Bishop Meade, an Episcopal clergyman of Virginia, who writes a book of sermons and tracts, specially intended to reconcile slaves to their condition. In the whole range of literature, there is perhaps nothing to match the following address, in which is

judicial blindness, and pharisaical malignity, to be denounced as an imposture; and that such a "revival" is only a device of time-serving hirelings to withdraw attention from the reforms of the age, and especially from the anti-slavery movement; to affect a zeal for God for the benefit of their craft; and to shield themselves from the condemnation which they deserve for their treachery to the rights of man. Resolved, That the charge brought by abolitionists against the northern church, that it is the bulwark of American slavery, finds its justification in much that transpires in what are denominated the religious anniversary meetings ; and as a special illustration of our meaning, we would point to the prayer-meeting in the Winter Street Church, which was opened with prayer by the Rev. Nehemiah Adams—a man standing before the world as the confessed champion of slavery, and yet retaining the unimpaired confidence and fellowship of the evangelical (so-called) churches.'

systematically perverted one of the clearest Christian injunctions. Speaking very solemnly, the bishop proceeds:

'When people die, we know of but two places they have to go to; and one is heaven, the other hell. Now, heaven is a place of great happiness, which God has prepared for all that are good, where they shall enjoy rest from their labours. And hell is a place of great torment and misery, where all wicked people will be shut up with the devil and other evil spirits, and be punished for ever, because they will not serve God. If, therefore, we would have our souls saved by Christ, if we would escape hell, and obtain heaven, we must set about doing what he requires of us—that is, to serve God. Your own poor circumstances in this life ought to put you particularly upon this and taking care of your souls. . . . . Almighty God hath been pleased to make you slaves here, and to give you nothing but labour and poverty in this world, which you are obliged to submit to, as it is His will that it should be so. And think within yourselves what a terrible thing it would be, after all your labours and sufferings in this life, to be turned into hell in the next life, and, after wearing out your bodies in service here, to go into a far worse slavery when this is over, and your poor souls be delivered over into the possession of the devil, to become his slaves for ever in hell, without any hope of ever getting free from it! If, therefore, you would be God's freemen in heaven, you must strive to be good and serve Him here on earth. Your bodies, you know, are not your own; they are at the disposal of those you belong to; but your precious souls are still your own, which nothing can take from you, if it be not your own fault. Consider well, then, that if you lose your souls by leading idle, wicked lives here, you have got nothing by it in this world, and you have lost your all in the next. For your idleness and wickedness are generally found out, and your bodies suffer for it here; and what is far worse, if you do not repent and amend, your unhappy souls will suffer for it hereafter.

'Having thus shewn you the chief duties you owe to your great Master in heaven, I now come to lay before you the duties you owe to your masters and mistresses here upon earth. And for this you have one general rule, that you ought always to carry in your minds, and that is, to *do all service for them as if you did it for God himself.* Poor creatures! you little consider when you are idle and neglectful of your masters' business; when you steal, and waste, and hurt any of their substance; when you are saucy and impudent; when you are telling them lies and deceiving them; or when you prove stubborn and sullen, and will not do the work you are set about without stripes and vexation—you do not consider, I say, that what faults you are guilty of towards your masters and mistresses, are faults done against God himself, who hath set your masters and mistresses over you in His own stead, and expects that you will do for them just as you would do for Him. And pray do not think that I want to deceive you when I tell you that your *masters and mistresses are God's overseers*, and that, if you are faulty towards them, God himself will punish you severely for it in the next world, unless you *repent* of it, and strive to make amends by your faithfulness and diligence for the time to come; for God himself hath declared the same.

'And in the first place, you are to be obedient and subject to your masters in all things. . . . . "*All things whatsoever ye would that men should do unto you, do ye even so unto them;*" that is, do by all mankind just as you would desire they should do by you, if you were in their place, and they in yours.

'Now, to suit this rule to your particular circumstances. Suppose you were masters and mistresses, and had servants under you, would you not desire that your servants should do their business *faithfully* and *honestly* as well when your back was turned as while you were looking over them? Would you not expect that they should take notice of what you said to them, that they should behave themselves with respect towards you and yours, and be as careful of everything belonging to you as you would be yourselves? You are servants: do, therefore, as you would wish to be done by, and you will be both good servants to your masters, and good servants to God, who requires this of you, and will reward you well for it, if you do it for the sake of conscience, in obedience to His commands. . . . . Take care that you do not fret, or murmur, or grumble at your condition; for this will not only make your life uneasy, but will greatly offend Almighty God. Consider that it is not yourselves—it is not the people you belong to—it is not the men that have brought you to it, but it is the will of God, who hath by His providence made you servants, because, no doubt, He knew that condition would be best for you in this world, and help you the better towards heaven, if you would but do your duty in it. So that any discontent at your not being free, or rich, or great, as you see some others, is quarrelling with your heavenly Master, and finding fault with God himself. . . . . There is only one circumstance which may appear grievous that I shall now take notice of; and that is CORRECTION.

'Now, when *correction* is given you, you either deserve it, or you do not deserve it. But whether you really deserve it or not, it is your duty, and Almighty God requires, that you bear it patiently. You may, perhaps, think that this is hard doctrine; but if you consider it rightly, you must needs think otherwise of it. Suppose, then, that you deserve correction; you cannot but say that it is just and right you should meet with it. Suppose you do not, or at least you do not deserve so much or so severe a correction for the fault you have committed; you perhaps have escaped a great many more, and are at least paid for all. Or suppose you are quite innocent of what is laid to your charge, and suffer wrongfully in that particular thing; is it not possible you may have done some other bad thing which was never discovered, and that Almighty God, who saw you doing it, would not let you escape without punishment one time or another? And ought you not in such a case to give glory to Him, and be thankful that He would rather punish you in this life for your wickedness, than destroy your souls for it in the next life? But suppose that even this was not the case—a case hardly to be imagined—and that you have by no means, known or unknown, deserved the correction you suffered; there is this great comfort in it, that if you bear it patiently, and leave your cause in the hands of God, he will reward you for it in heaven, and the punishment you suffer unjustly here shall turn to your exceeding great glory hereafter.'

All that need be said is—after this, anything! Mrs Stowe (*Key to Uncle Tom's Cabin*) observes that such discourses only 'shew how perfectly use may familiarise amiable and estimable men with a system of oppression, till they shall have lost all consciousness of the wrong which it involves.' The bishop, she adds, has since emancipated all his slaves.

By way of variety, we shall conclude with a quotation from a recent work, entitled *The Hireling and the Slave*, by William J. Grayson, published at Charleston, South Carolina, 1856. Mr Grayson is a poet who devotes his muse to the praise of southern institutions; and thinks, with Dr Rice, that the negro is brought to America for wisely providential purposes, and that nothing can equal the comforts of his position as a slave. Here is his picture:

'And yet the life, so unassailed by care,
So blessed with moderate work, with ample fare,
With all the good the starving pauper needs
The happier slave on each plantation leads;
Safe from harassing doubts and annual fears,
He dreads no famine in unfruitful years;

If harvests fail, from inauspicious skies,
The master's providence his food supplies;
No paupers perish here for want of bread,
Or lingering live, by foreign bounty fed;
No exiled trains of homeless peasants go,
In distant climes to tell their tales of wo:
Far other fortune, free from care and strife,
For work, or bread, attends the negro's life,
And Christian slaves may challenge as their own,
The blessings claimed in fabled states alone—
The cabin home, not comfortless though rude,
Light daily labour, and abundant food,
The sturdy health that temperate habits yield,
The cheerful song that rings in every field,
The long, loud laugh, that freemen seldom share,
Heaven's boon to bosoms unapproached by care,
And boisterous jest and humour unrefined,
That leave, though rough, no painful sting behind;
While, nestling near, to bless their humble lot,
Warm social joys surround the negro's cot,
The evening dance its merriment imparts,
Love, with its rapture, fills their youthful hearts,
And placid age, the task of labour done,
Enjoys the summer shade, the winter sun,
And, as through life no pauper want he knows,
Laments no poor-house penance at its close.'

Mr Grayson subsequently tells his mind freely about the whole tribe of fault-finders with slavery. Mrs Stowe comes in for a large share of coarse abuse.

ECONOMIC VIEW OF THE SUBJECT.

THE number of slaves in the United States in 1850, as formerly stated, was 3,204,313. The ratio of increase differs greatly in different states. While very rapid in the more southern, it is comparatively small in the more northern slave states; the explanation of this being, that there is a breeding and a consuming set of states. The increase of slaves in the whole slave states, was, between 1790 and 1800, 27·9 per cent.; between 1800 and 1810, 33·4 per cent.; between 1810 and 1820, 29·1 per cent.; between 1820 and 1830, 30·6 per cent.; between 1830 and 1840, 28·8 per cent.—the average of all these ratios being 28·96 per cent. These statistics are given in a well-digested compendium of official documents, by Messrs Chase and Sanborn,* who proceed to say: 'In 1840, the slave-exporting states, Delaware, Maryland, Virginia, North and South Carolina, Kentucky, and Tennessee, contained 1,479,601 slaves. Had they increased in the ratio of 28·96 per cent., the number in 1850 would have been 1,908,093. The actual number given is 1,689,158, being a difference of 218,935, or 21,893 for each year to be accounted for. Applying the same rule to the slave-importing states, we have the following result: Georgia, Florida, Alabama, Louisiana, Mississippi, Arkansas, and Missouri contained, in 1840, 1,002,031 slaves. Increasing in the ratio of 28·96 per cent., their

* *The North and the South; a Statistical View of the Condition of the Free and the Slave States.* By Henry Chase and Charles W. Sanborn. Boston: 1856.

number in 1850 would have been 1,292,219. The number given in the census is 1,453,035; a difference *the other way* of 160,816, or 16,081 per year, which they had received by importation. The difference of nearly 6000 between the import and export may be accounted for by the following: a writer in the *New Orleans Argus,* in 1830, says—"The loss by death in bringing slaves from a northern climate, which our planters are under the necessity of doing, is not less than 25 per cent." And the planters in those states, when advertising for sale a plantation and a lot of negroes, always mention distinctly the fact that they are "acclimated"—if that be the case—as enhancing their value.'

According to the best information, the number of slaves annually sold from the breeding to the consuming states is estimated at 25,000. As regards the value of this amount of 'stock,' a conjecture may be hazarded. The price-list furnished to me by a dealer at Richmond in 1853, stated the value of 'best men 18 to 25 years old,' to be 1200 to 1300 dollars; 'fair ditto,' 950 to 1050; 'boys 4 feet 5 inches high,' 500 to 600; 'girls 5 feet high,' 750 to 850; and 'girls of 4 feet,' 350 to 432. Since that time, slaves have considerably risen in price, and are continually rising, in consequence of the increasing demand for cotton. The average value of male and female negroes raised for export, might now be moderately set down at 600 dollars, at which price the total market-value of the 25,000 slaves sent southward every year is 15,000,000 dollars. The negroes exported are usually between the ages of 10 and 25; neither infants nor old persons being available for the purpose. The trader, also, leaves a residuum of defective stock, which although fed, doctored, and dressed up for sale, cannot easily be disposed of, even at very reduced prices.

I learned in America that there are quack-doctors skilful in giving a sleek and robust appearance to negroes in poor health; but from the sharp scrutiny which I saw exercised by the buyers at public auctions, I should imagine it to be much more difficult to push off a faulty negro than a faulty horse.

Taking old and young, of every quality, the average value of slaves is quoted by Chase and Sanborn at 400 dollars each; and on the basis of this calculation, the entire value of the slaves in the slave states, in 1850, was 1,280,145,600 dollars. The value of the farms in the slave states in the same year was 1,117,649,649 dollars — excess in value of slaves over lands, 162,495,951 dollars. The number of slaveholders in the slave states, in 1850, was 346,048. If each of the slaveholders be valued at the average price of his slaves (400 dollars), the united value of lands and owners will be 1,256,068,849 dollars, or a little less than the value of the slaves. 'Thus,' observe our authorities, 'has the industry and political and domestic economy of the slaveholders, in two hundred and thirty years, been able to bring the value of their lands and themselves nearly up to the market-value of their slaves; and all three together—lands, slaves, and slaveholders—to nearly half the value of the property of the free states.'

The contrast between the northern and southern states is strongly brought out. In 1850, the value of real and personal estate in the free states was 4,107,162,198 dollars; the value of real and personal estate in the slave states, 2,936,090,737 dollars; but deducting value of slaves, as above, the true value in slave states was 1,655,945,137. The whole area of the free states is 392,062,080 acres, and value of real and personal estate, in 1850, 10 dollars 47 cents per acre. The area of the slave states is 544,926,720 acres, and value of real and personal estate per acre, in 1850, 3 dollars and 4 cents per acre. According to fresh statistical returns in 1856, the value of real and personal estate in the free states had then risen to 14 dollars 72 cents per acre, and the value of the real and personal estate in the slave states had reached only 4 dollars 59 cents per acre. The valuation of the state of New York, in 1855, was 1,401,285,279 dollars—a sum greater than the whole value of the slave states in 1850. The value of real and personal estate of Massachusetts, in 1850, was more than that (slaves excepted) of the states of Virginia, North and South Carolina, Georgia, Florida, and Texas. Massachusetts measures 4,992,000 acres; the six slave states just mentioned measure 317,576,320 acres. In Massachusetts, the value of real and personal estate per acre was 114 dollars 85 cents per acre; the value of the real and personal estate in these six slave states was 1 dollar 81 cents per acre. In fact, says the authority before us, 'Massachusetts is able to buy and pay for considerably more than half the great empire of slavery, and have more money left than the Pilgrims landed with at Plymouth; while Pennsylvania could easily buy out the other half.'

It is further shewn, from a close analysis of facts, that the effects of slavery and freedom on the value of adjacent lands is reciprocal—the proximity of slavery lessening the value in the free states, and the neighbourhood of freedom raising the value in the slave states. The abolition of slavery would in a few years more than treble the value of all the lands of the slave states now under culture; and by such increase of value, any loss by emancipation would more than compensate for the sacrifice. All this is proved beyond a doubt by figures.

The contrast between North and South, with respect

to education, libraries, and other agencies of social improvement, is not less striking. Not to tire with dry statistics, we shall present only a few of the more remarkable particulars. The number of public schools in the slave states is 18,507; in the free states, 62,433. Number of scholars in slave states, 581,861; in free states, 2,769,901. In the slave states, there are in private academies and schools, 104,976 scholars. But comparing the number of pupils at public and private establishments, North and South, the free states have a majority of 2,241,046, being three times the entire number attending school in the slave states. The money expended annually on schools in the slave states is 4,799,258 dollars; and in the free states, 9,237,709 dollars. Ohio, a free state, is not quite two-thirds as large as Virginia; Virginia has 77,764 scholars, and Ohio has 502,826. Virginia has been settled upwards of two centuries; Ohio, about sixty years since. Virginia occupies one of the finest situations in the world, on the coast of the Atlantic; Ohio is a thousand miles inland. In 1854, Virginia expended for the education of poor children, 69,404 dollars; for the maintenance of a public guard, 73,189 dollars. The New-England States, with an area less than one-twelfth greater, appropriated 2,000,000 dollars for public schools, and felt secure without a guard. In the same year, Kentucky expended on public schools, 146,047 dollars; Ohio, adjoining it, appropriated 2,266,609 dollars. The number of native white citizens who cannot read or write, in the free states, is 248,725; and in the slave states, 493,026—a number about twice as great, in a population of far less than half. The number of native white adults who cannot read and write, in Tennessee, is 77,017, in a white population of 756,836; the number in New York, 23,241, in a white population of 3,048,325. In

Virginia, there are 75,868 native whites over twenty years of age who can neither read nor write; North Carolina, 73,226; Georgia, 40,794; Kentucky, 64,340. The number of white inhabitants in the state of New Hampshire is 174,232. Among these, the number of native adults who cannot read and write is 893, or 1 in 201; in Connecticut, it is 1 in 277; in Vermont, 1 in 284; in Massachusetts, 1 in 517. Applying the same test to the slave states—in South Carolina it is 1 in 7; in Virginia, 1 in 5; in North Carolina, 1 in 3.

The total number of volumes in the public libraries in the slave states, is 649,577; in those of the free states, 3,888,234—6 to 1. The Sunday-school libraries of the North are nearly twice as great as all the college libraries of the South. The very small state of Rhode Island has more volumes in her libraries than Virginia. The daily press of the South issues 47,000,000 copies annually; the North, 181,000,000 copies annually. One New York paper has a circulation about half as large as all the daily papers of the slave states. The number of copies of scientific papers printed in the slave states is 372,000; in Massachusetts alone, the number is 2,000,000—more than five times as many.

Chase and Sanborn give some useful explanations concerning representation. 'The number of free inhabitants in the slave states is 6,412,605; and in the free states, 13,434,686. The number of freemen in the free states is, therefore, over 600,000 *more than double* the number in the slave states. The representation in congress is, from the slave states, ninety members, representing the 6,000,000; and from the free states, 144, representing the 13,000,000. This discrepancy between population and representation arises from the fact that, in determining the number of representatives to which each state is entitled, five slaves are reckoned equal to three freemen. The 3,200,304 slaves, therefore, in the slave states are reckoned equal to 1,920,182⅔ freemen, and are represented accordingly. The slaves of the South have, therefore, a representation equal to that of the free states of New Hampshire, Vermont, Connecticut, Iowa, and Wisconsin. Without the representation allowed to slave property, the number of representatives from the slave states would be 75, instead of 90; and from the free states, 159, instead of 144—a gain of 80 in favour of the free states; making their representation double that of the slave states, even without the representation of Rhode Island, Wisconsin, California, and Iowa. It will be seen that in the late severe contests in the House of Representatives, had freemen only been represented, the question would invariably have been decided in favour of the North.'

Of the 346,048 slaveholders in the slave states, it appears from the census tables, that '173,204 hold less than five slaves, leaving 172,844 who are holders of more than four slaves; and if we deduct the numbers holding less than ten slaves, there will remain 92,215. The whole number of slaveholders, then, is less than 350,000, including females and minors. The number of voters in this class is therefore much smaller,' shewing an immense balance in favour of the North, in point of power at elections.

Then, take agricultural produce, there is the same preponderance in favour of the North. In 1850, the value of the agricultural produce in the free states was 358,634,334 dollars, or 342 dollars per head; in the slave states, 631,277,417 dollars, or 171 dollars per head. 'The North,' adds our authority, 'with half as much land under cultivation, and two-thirds as many persons engaged in farming, produces 227,000,000 dollars' worth of agricultural produce in a year more than the South; twice as much on an acre, and more than double the value per head of every person engaged in farming.' This occurs, while the South paying nothing in the form of wages for labour, has better land, a monopoly of cotton, rice, cane-sugar, and nearly so of tobacco and hemp, with above all, a climate yielding two, and sometimes three, crops in a year.

Compare South and North in the matter of manufactures. In the slave states, the capital employed in manufactures is 64,196,736 dollars; hands employed, 104,101; annual product, 95,116,284 dollars. As regards the free states, the capital invested is 467,015,720 dollars; hands employed, 838,212; the annual product, 942,882,801 dollars. The value of the products which enter into the commerce of the two sections, in 1850, was, for free states, 1,377,199,968 dollars; slave states, 410,754,992 dollars. While the North employs in commerce 188,271 hands, the South employs 70,165. The length of railroads in the free states in 1854 was 13,105 miles; slave states, 4212 miles. Canals in free states, 3682 miles; slave states, 1116 miles. In 1855, the tonnage of vessels was five times as much in the North as in the South. The tonnage built this year in Massachusetts was 79,670 tons; in South Carolina, 61 tons. The tonnage built in Maine alone was four times greater than that built in the whole slave states. Even of that built in the South, the tonnage is the work of northern and foreign mechanics. In the case of a dissolution of the Union, and hostilities between the North and South, the highest naval science, and large amount of capital, would need to be called into requisition by the South, in order to protect its seven thousand miles of exposed sea-coast.

The South is continually projecting schemes for extending commerce, manufactures, literature, everything; but national wealth is not a result of talk, but of combined intelligence and industry. An English traveller fears that the South will aggravate its peculiar institutions by employing slaves in manufactures. Such apprehensions are groundless. Skilled labour infers education, and that is totally irreconcilable with slavery, by maintaining which, the South restricts itself to the rudest kind of unskilled operations, leaves the finest water-power in the world unused, places itself in a condition of dependence on northern ingenuity.

The extent of correspondence by letters is usually an indication of the degree of mental and commercial activity. It appears that the amount paid for postages in the South does not pay expenses of transportation by over 800,000 dollars, while the free-state postages more than pay expenses by over 2,000,000 dollars. The slave states get their letters carried at the expense of the free states, which pay their own expenses besides. The value of the churches in the slave states is 21,674,581 dollars; in the free states, 67,773,477 dollars. The churches in New York equal in value all the churches in the fifteen slave states.

These are instructive particulars. They conclusively shew the relative inferior position of the South; and the wonder grows how a section of the Union which has so little to boast of, should have had the address to obtain supreme command. Political supremacy, however, cannot compensate for social decay. As almost every natural aptitude for prosperity is in favour of the South, the only reasonable explanation of the backward condition revealed by statistics, is the blight of slavery. On that, if the South were wise, its mind should rest. Judiciously disregarding all extraneous circumstances, we can imagine that its true course would be to consider whether slavery, though possibly advantageous to a limited number of individuals, is not an insurmountable obstacle to general prosperity. Not alone from official statistics, but from a variety of details gathered from other sources, we can see that slavery is an error in social economics, independently of its moral pollutions.

Slavery, as has been stated, gradually disappeared in the northern states, by the plan of allowing the slaves to die out; all born after a certain date being free. We observe, by the census tables, that as lately as 1820, there were in Rhode Island 48 slaves; Connecticut, 97; New York, 10,088; New Jersey, 7657. In 1830, there were in Rhode Island 17; Connecticut, 25; New York, 75; New Jersey, 2254. In 1840, there were in Rhode Island 5; Connecticut, 17; New York, 4; New Jersey, 674. Advancing to 1850, the whole had died out in Rhode Island, Connecticut, and New York, and there remained in New Jersey only 236, in the character of apprentices. Slavery was abolished in New York in 1825, and this act of justice and humanity may be said to have taken place from a deliberate conviction that there could be no sound prosperity or social advancement so long as the institution lasted. Of the change effected by emancipation, we have some account in the work of the late Mr Johnston, who visited the States on an agricultural tour a few years ago.* This intelligent observer resided for some days with Dr Beekman at Kinderhook on the Hudson; and his host, referring to the times of slavery, mentioned the following circumstances, to which we call the attention of gentlemen in the slave states generally, and more particularly those in Maryland, Virginia, and Kentucky:

'Those were the times when only the blacks laboured. The white man considered himself above labour. The

---

* *Notes on North America.* By J. F. W. Johnston, Lecturer on Chemistry, University of Durham. 2 vols. 1851.

work of the slaves had to support the white man and his family, besides themselves and their own families. With the useless mouths to feed, and useless backs to clothe, he was considered a successful farmer who could make both ends meet.

'It was then the custom for the white men, both old and young, of a neighbourhood, by eleven o'clock in the morning, to collect at the nearest public-houses. In many townships there were scores of these, and Kinderhook had its share. Here they remained talking and drinking till early dinner-time, returned again by five in the afternoon, and spent the evening, till probably midnight, in drinking, gambling, cock-fighting, horse-racing, or perhaps fighting among themselves. Idleness led the way to immorality, and to frequent ruin on the part of the whites.

'But when the abolition of slavery came—"Who will till our farms?" it was asked; "we shall all be ruined." But gradually good sense overcame prejudice. The freed blacks were at first hired as labourers, but white labour gradually took its place —and now "the dignity of labour" is the watchword of a powerful party in the confederation. The sons of the farmer, instead of spending their time in idleness and dissipation, from a kind of necessity, became first producers, and afterwards intelligent interested improvers. Old uncomfortable houses gave way to new and commodious ones. The outbuildings were enlarged, improved, and made ornamental. Waste land has been brought into cultivation; fences erected that will secure the crops; the stock changed into objects of beauty as well as profit; roads, bridges, schoolhouses, and churches completed—all these things are creditable to us, as we are now an industrious, thriving, intelligent, moral, and religious people. Such I have seen to be the fruits of free labour; and whereas in those days money to borrow could scarcely be met with, I know that the rural population of 4000, now living round this place, have at least a million of dollars lent, and at interest. This is the fearful ordeal which the growers of wheat by slave-labour, in Maryland and Virginia, dread to encounter; though experience proves it to be the sure way to independence, comfort, and wealth.'

Are we to assume that, for the sake of exporting fifteen millions of dollars' worth of negroes, annually, from Virginia and adjacent states, slavery is inflicted like a chronic disease on the community? It is, we believe, at least undeniable, that but for the power exercised by slave breeders and dealers, Virginia would speedily be added to the number of free states. Olmsted says there are in Virginia 'a very large number of voters, strongly desirous, either from selfish or other motives, that the state should be free from slavery.' But no candidate who advocated freedom, would be allowed to open his mouth publicly on the subject. All the ordinary means of collecting assemblages would be denied him; all the newspapers, bar-room orators, and clergy would be against him; and the poor traders and mechanics, fearful of offending their customers, would not dare to support him. Thus, local efforts to suppress slavery are, in present circumstances, impracticable.

Mr Olmsted compares the start in life of a farmer in the free state of Iowa, and that of a planter in Texas. Each has the same amount of capital. The Iowan hires his labour, buys the best implements, and, besides, contributes to the construction of churches, schools, railways, and other public works. The Texan sinks his capital in buying negroes, and is embarrassed at the outset. He can help forward no improvements, can buy no improved implements, but must employ 'such rude substitutes as his stupid, uninstructed, and uninterested slaves can readily make in his ill-furnished plantation workshop.' It is true, the keep of the slaves is less than the wages paid to the free workmen; yet, this is an illusory benefit. The planter has to support old and young, occasionally lose a slave by death or escape, and he lives in a moral desert, terribly annoyed with his servants, whom he declares to be the laziest rascals in existence. The Iowan hires only those hands whom he really wants. The wages he gives them are spent in the neighbourhood, and form a fund for all kinds of public and private improvements. By means of these improvements—railways, for example —the whole operations of the free-state farmer are facilitated. His outlays return to him fourfold. He is at ease; the minds of his children are not tainted by the sights and sounds which accompany slavery. If the Texan gets rich in slaves, he has few public advantages; and just as he attains opulence, he finds that his lands are becoming exhausted, and that the produce of labour is sensibly diminishing.

The answer of the planters to remonstrances against slavery would of course be, that by no other means could their sugar, rice, or cotton plantations be cultivated—there is no body of free labourers, supposing that free labour was desirable—were the slaves emancipated, they would not work for hire, and consequently would become a nuisance, as the North declares the free coloured population to be. We can suppose that such would be the aggregate answer; for we have repeatedly seen something of the kind in the southern newspapers. The answer is worthy of more calm consideration from the opponents of slavery than it has usually received.

To fortify its argument, the South appeals to the case of the planters in the British West Indies; ruined, as they allege, by emancipation. The West

Indian proprietary was in an unwholesome condition in 1833, perhaps as bad as was the Irish proprietary, until rectified by the Encumbered Estates Court. Possibly, the southern proprietary, take it all in all, is not much better, as we hear occasionally of northern holders of mortgages—New York merchants, probably standing in the same relation to Louisiana as did those of Liverpool and London to Jamaica. So far, then, there is perhaps some analogy between the financial position of American and British West Indian planters. That emancipation greatly dislocated labour in the West Indies, is beyond a doubt; nor could such a sudden change take place without less or more social disturbance. The plans of gradual emancipation pursued in the Northern states were, however, attended with so little difficulty to farmers, notwithstanding their fears on the subject, as ought to convince the South that processes of emancipation are not in all circumstances ruinous.

In the bountifulness of a sub-tropical climate, we are aware that persons of idle habits, reared under forced labour, will be inclined to depend more on simple natural products for subsistence than on settled wages. But from this state of demoralisation there is a rebound, as is instanced in the British colonies. *Things right themselves at last.* On this point, we cannot do better than offer some remarks which lately appeared in an ably conducted print, the *Anti-slavery Advocate*: *

'The impression, we believe, prevails among the American planters, that the British West Indies are rapidly returning to a state of nature; and especially are fast abandoning the sugar-cane, as too much for the energies of free labour. Happily, the commercial

---

* Number for February 1857. Tweedie, Strand, London.

returns dispel this ridiculous illusion. Slavery was abolished by the Act of 1833; the system of forced labour being still continued for some years under the name of apprenticeship, and the monopoly by differential duties remaining unbroken until 1845. If we take the produce of the three years 1835, 1845, and 1855, we shall see at a glance, 1*st*, The latest achievements of the slave system with protection duties; 2*dly*, The result of free labour without free trade; and 3*dly*, The most recent operation of a system doubly free. In the first of the three selected years, our slave colonies (West Indies and Mauritius) furnished for home consumption only, 178,000 tons of sugar and molasses; in the second, 180,626; in the third, 211,631. Thus the free produce, instead of dwindling away in obedience to prediction, has increased about 19 per cent. Still, while defending the results of the great British experiment from misapprehension, we are far from denying that the curse of slavery has been redeemed by vast effort and sacrifice. Nor could it be removed from the adjacent continent without still greater and more protracted loss, during the transition to a better system. Under slavery alone do men exist for the mere soil's sake. With freedom, nature reasserts her rights, and the soil is found to exist for the sake of men: and as in Jamaica, so in America, the labourer, left at his own disposal, will be content with the kind and degree of work which suffices to supply his customary wants. It is not reasonable to expect from the African, trained in the worship of idleness, a spontaneous and superfluous industry. The energy which only the competition of numbers extorts from a white peasantry, will reserve itself for the same stimulus among the coloured races.' The writer candidly adds, that it would be 'a waste of time to discuss the relative *cheapness or dearness* of free labour under conditions which tempt it to retire from market altogether. Such conditions, we fear, are present over a large area in the southern states, and constrain us to admit a powerful, though not permanent, economic interest in favour of the existing system.'*

The South is, happily, not without examples of successful free rural labour within the slave states. There are now flourishing colonies of New Englanders and other settlers in Western Virginia, Scotch in Georgia, and more particularly Germans in Texas—these latter already considerable in numbers. We shall immediately call attention to the account of a thriving German settlement given by Mr Olmsted, who visited it in 1856. The same writer has done good service to his country in describing the industrial arrangements on a large rice-plantation in Georgia, belonging to a Mr X——, whose treatment of his 'servants' is of the most exemplary kind. To all the slaves, tasks are assigned according to their ability. The tasks are so moderate, that many finish their labour at three or four o'clock in the afternoon; and they can employ the remainder of the day in labouring for themselves. They are allowed half-acre lots of land, besides a garden, to cultivate on their own behalf. They are likewise at liberty to keep swine and fowls. All they do not need for themselves, they sell. The family of Mr X—— have no other supply

* 'At a meeting held in the Mansion House, London, January 5, 1857, for the purpose of presenting a testimonial to Dr Livingstone, Mr Montgomery Martin stated that he had recently visited the West Indies, to ascertain if the emancipation of the slaves had produced ruin there. "He found there a free, happy, and prosperous population; and, speaking commercially, the West Indies now yielded more rum, sugar, and other produce, than it had ever done during the existence of slavery. Since the abolition of slavery in the West Indies, not a drop of blood was shed—not a single crime was committed—nor was there any destruction of property throughout the whole of the West Indies."'

of poultry and eggs than what is so obtained from their own negroes; they also purchase game from them. By these various means, the slaves realise money, and actually become creditors of their master. At the time of Mr Olmsted's visit, Mr X—— owed his slaves 1500 dollars.

The picture here presented is truly suggestive. We are sure our readers will be glad to see the result at which Mr Olmsted arrives. 'The ascertained practicability of thus dealing with slaves, together with the obvious advantages of the method of working them by tasks, which I have described, seem to me to indicate that it is not so impracticable as is generally supposed, if only it was desired by those having the power, to rapidly extinguish slavery, and while doing so, to educate the negro for taking care of himself, in freedom. ' Let, for instance, any slave be provided with all things he will demand, as far as practicable, and charge him for them at certain prices—honest, market prices for his necessities, higher prices for harmless luxuries, and excessive, but not absolutely prohibitory, prices for everything likely to do him harm. Credit him, at a fixed price, for every day's work he does, and for all above a certain easily accomplished task in a day, at an increased price, so that his reward will be in an increasing ratio to his perseverance. Let the prices of provisions be so proportioned to the price of taskwork, that it will be about as easy as it is now for him to obtain a bare subsistence. When he has no food and shelter due him, let him be confined in solitude, or otherwise punished, until he asks for opportunity to earn exemption from punishment by labour.

'When he desires to marry, and can persuade any woman to marry him, let the two be dealt with as in partnership. Thus, a young man or young woman will be attractive, somewhat in proportion to his or her reputation for industry and providence. Thus industry and providence will become fashionable. Oblige them to purchase food for their children, and let them have the benefit of their children's labour, and they will be careful to teach their children to avoid waste, and to honour labour. Let those who have not gained credit while hale and young, sufficient to support themselves in comfort when prevented by age or infirmity from further labour, be supported by a tax upon all the negroes of the plantation, or of a community. Improvidence, and pretence of inability to labour, will then be disgraceful.

'When any man has a balance to his credit equal to his value as a slave, let that constitute him a free man. It will be optional with him and his employer, whether he shall continue longer in the relation of servant. If desirable for both that he should, it is probable that he will; for unless he is honest, prudent, industrious, and discreet, he will not have acquired the means of purchasing his freedom.'

Our author adds, that such a system would partake of the emancipation law of Cuba, where, he says, 'every slave has the privilege of emancipating himself, by paying a price which does not depend upon the selfish exactions of the masters; but it is either a fixed price, or else is fixed, in each case, by disinterested appraisers. The consequence is, that emancipations are constantly going on, and the free people of colour are becoming enlightened, cultivated, and wealthy. In no part of the United States do they occupy the high social position which they enjoy in Cuba.'

It is exceedingly to be regretted, that the South, for whatever reason, should reject explanations on matters of this kind; for from the facts above advanced from credible authorities, the planters do themselves less than justice by the course they have hitherto thought fit to pursue. Perhaps they unite in the common belief, that cotton could not possibly be cultivated by free white labour. Olmsted's description of the German colony of New-Braunfels, in Texas, puts this notion to flight. He found hundreds of small farms on which cotton was cultivated year after year by white farmers and their families—'the result, a total of 800 bales, which, at Galveston, brought from one to two cents a pound more than that produced by slaves, owing to the more careful handling of white and personally interested labour.' He adds, that these 800 bales, though a drop in the bucket to the whole crop, are a very substantial evidence of the possibilities of not only white, but well-regulated free labour in the South.'

We can readily understand that the present urgent demand for cotton, indisposes planters to run any risks in exchanging slave for free black, and it may be, free white labour. They must at the same time feel, however, that their tenure of slave-property is far from secure—that they sleep on a volcano, which may any day overwhelm them and their possessions—or, at the very least, that, from revelations recently made of southern policy, the sentiments of every civilised nation are setting more steadily against them.

There are other considerations. We have reason to believe that a considerable and steadily directed effort will speedily be made, in Great Britain, to procure supplies of cotton from India and Africa, where, by means of cheap labour, improved machinery, railways, English capital, and other advantages, it is hoped that the cotton produce will rise materially in quantity and quality. This effort arises from no bad feeling towards American planters, but from the circumstance, that they cannot send us a sufficient supply of cotton, great as that is— 1,758,301 bags in 1856; the total consumption of all kinds of cotton in Great Britain, per annum, being 2,468,160 packages, and more wanted. It is not expected that the demand for the finer kinds of American cotton will be lessened; yet, the successful opening of fresh fields of culture could hardly fail to act in the usual way of competition, by lowering prices, and ultimately diverting trade into new channels. The anti-slavery party in England look with no little interest on this movement.

The reader has been conducted through a history—such as it is—of American slavery, and been made acquainted with some prominent features in its character. He perceives that, as a carefully nourished institution, it imparts a tone to the whole social system of the United States, interweaves itself with the national constitution, laws, usages, sentiments, the most vital principles of public polity.

Though marvellous in many respects, this institution has not seemingly attained its full proportions. It is still growing. Sixty-seven years ago, under a million—now approaching five millions—soon there will be ten millions of human beings in the condition of 'chattels personal'—a nation of slaves within a nation of freemen, a people dangerous in their numbers and sense of wrongs, dangerous as an engine of intestine discord, in the event of hostilities with an unscrupulous foreign enemy.

Can no practicable measures be devised to arrest this monster evil in its desolating course? We may be better able to reply to this inquiry after glancing at the causes which have conspired to bring about present results.

First, and at the foundation of the whole mischief, lie the provisions of the federal constitution, which, as formerly shewn, pledge the whole states to maintain slavery inviolate in any individual state where it exists—which authorise a method of representation in the House of Representatives, based on a certain numerical proportion of slaves; whereby the southern faction gains thirty votes—and which, by giving national efficacy to a fugitive slave law, bring the whole country within the operation of southern institutions.

Practically, the constitution of the United States is incapable of change. To amend it, there would need to be a very effective rousing of public feeling throughout the various states. Congress must be besieged with petitions—which would have little effect, constituted as that body now is. Supposing this difficulty to be overcome, a proposal for amendment must be concurred in by two-thirds of both branches of congress—hopeless. Supposing this difficulty also overcome, conventions to take the matter into consideration must be called by the legislatures of the several states. Lastly, the decision of the conventions must be ratified by three-fourths of the states; by which is inferred the consent of six of the slave states—hopeless. To all appearance, therefore, reform is constitutionally impossible.

Second. With such constitutional advantages in its favour, as well as by superior address, the southern party has obtained such political supremacy, as enables it to secure northern votes. Having thus a majority in congress, it has from time to time, by legislative measures, extended slavery over newly acquired territories; and judging from recent elections, it has now a greater power of doing so than ever.

Third. Northern selfishness, by which freedom and independence are bartered for place, pay, commercial monopoly, and other material interests.

Fourth—although this might almost be placed first—There is the universal desire to support the Union, which, having attained great eminence and glory, is, right or wrong, idolised to a very extraordinary degree.

Fifth. Fears of destroying this object of worship, along with the blinding effects of political partisanship, produce a Public Opinion that acts despotically in suppressing freedom of speech; wherefore, all who express a detestation of slavery, and agitate for its restriction or extinction, are proscribed as 'abolitionists'—a name, in popular acceptation, synonymous with everything that is infamous.

Sixth. The propagation of corrupt doctrines by religious teachers of almost every denomination, to the effect that slavery is an institution beneficently designed by Providence for the spiritual welfare of its victims. And along with this agency may be classed the dissemination of pro-slavery sentiments, and the ridicule of anti-slavery efforts, by a great part of the press, which takes its tone from Public Opinion.

Seventh. The prejudice respecting colour throughout the greater part of the free states; and the notion, generally, that the negro is from nature of an inferior and servile race.

Eighth. The continually growing demand for cotton, before which every consideration of humanity, or dread of consequences, disappears.

Some other causes might be assigned; as, for example, party violence by mobs at elections, by which quietly disposed and respectable persons are driven from the field of politics, and power handed over to those who aim as much at selfish ends as the public advantage. And then, to account for these scenes of violence, as well as for much newspaper abuse, we might allude to the strange practice of discharging almost all government-officers and appointing new ones, according to political changes, by which a state of disorder is kept up in the country by all classes of office-seekers.

Out of this complication of causes, we leave any one to say how American slavery is to be alleviated. Congress has only a power of restraining it from entering the territories—and even this power is not undisputed. Slavery can be legally abolished only by the separate action of each individual state; and within each slave state there exists a dominating power, apparently impervious to any reasonable proposition on the subject. Not even the respective legislatures of these states could relax the slave code, without a very general consent of the people. In the matter of slavery, Vigilance Committees are above all law. And measures for emancipation, supposing them attempted, might be followed by revolution.

It is not to be supposed that an evil so conspicuous, so fraught with probabilities of mischief, and, to say the least of it, so damaging to the character of those by whom it is cherished, should have escaped the notice of Americans. But unfortunately, it has never attained the position of a public or generally discussed question—it seems as though an impression prevailed that nothing could be made of it, or that for certain reasons it was improper to speak of it at all. Slavery, in short, is a kind of tabooed subject in the States. It is not an agreeable thing to think of, certainly not to talk about.

When tourists, in their curiosity to arrive at the truth, refer to this grievous evil, they find little to put in their note-book. The best they get is the pious remark, 'that slavery is one of those sad evils which will doubtless pass away in God's own good time.' And, thus, worthy people consoling themselves with a highly edifying sentiment, go placidly to sleep, and leave slavery to take its chance. It must be deemed odd that this great people, renowned for their shrewdness, should for any reason shrink from the open discussion of a social question which so intimately concerns their welfare. 'Abolition' haunts them like a spectre. Let us have a look at this terrible apparition.

A number of years ago, there sprung up anti-slavery societies, differing considerably in their views. Some of the older associations have disappeared, others with more vitality have become permanent. The American Anti-slavery Society, located at New York, takes the lead among existing institutions. Massachusetts has several associations in vigorous operation, the chief one, as we believe, being called the Massachusetts Anti-slavery Society, which began in 1832, and holds annual festivals of much oratorical importance. This society was formed 'on the ground of the Absolute Sin of Slaveholding, and the Duty of Immediate and Unconditional Emancipation.' The president is William Lloyd Garrison; and among the office-bearers or adherents are other leading abolitionists — Wendell Phillips, Samuel May, Edmund Quincy, Maria M. Chapman, Lucy Stone, Lucretia Mott, and Theodore Parker. The abolitionists, represented by these and similar societies, will make no compromise on the subject of slavery; nor do they design to work through religious or political organisations. They declare, there is an inherent wickedness in slavery, with which there can be no association. It is not clear to us from their writings what is their plan for effecting 'immediate emancipation.' We presume, they merely insist that the whole of the slaves should be instantly liberated, without compensation to owners, and without any preparation, educational or otherwise, for the enjoyment of freedom. A number of the members are Non-resistants—a class of persons who repudiate the federal constitution, and decline to take any part in elections. Those who entertain these ultra views, desire to dissolve the Union, in order to be entirely rid of any connection with the South.

Next comes the Liberty party, which also advocates immediate emancipation, but does not think so badly of the constitution, and accordingly is opposed to a dissolution of the Union. Its members do not withdraw from their church relations, on account of slavery, and hope to effect their purposes by moderate means. Many of the party are connected with societies, which rely on the diffusion of religious knowledge in the South as one of the best plans for promoting anti-slavery sentiments in that quarter.

We believe the Liberty party is now pretty nearly swallowed up in the new Republican party. Europeans have heard much lately of the Republicans, and it is interesting to know what really is their anti-slavery doctrine. Properly speaking, they are not abolitionists at all. No doubt, many members would wish immediate emancipation, and their papers and orations in favour of liberty are unexceptionable. But the members generally are only Free-soilers. They disclaim any intention of meddling with slavery where it exists, and will be satisfied with seeing it kept out of the territories, which would doubtless be a great point gained. They do not advocate a dissolution of the Union; though it is not unlikely, should other projects fail, that they will come to that. They have confident anticipations of carrying a Republican as president in 1860, and live on in this hope. To this great political organisation belong Charles Sumner, Hall, Giddings, Chase, Henry Ward Beecher, Seward, and Horace Greeley.

Finally, we might mention the party called Union-savers, represented by Fillmore, who look upon slavery as a bad thing in principle, but deprecate all agitation on the subject. By lending themselves politically to the democrats, they sink the question of slavery altogether, and serve materially to impose that restraint on free opinion which is so injurious to the cause of freedom.

It will be observed that among these parties there

is only one entitled to be called true abolitionists; all the others postponing the question of emancipation, or subordinating it to certain political and religious considerations.

As a reason for persecuting abolitionists, it has been alleged that their object is to stir up mischief in the South; that by means of tracts and other agencies, they endeavour to spread incendiary doctrines, and place the owners of slaves in constant danger of insurrection and loss of property. It is further alleged, that the laws against teaching slaves to read, are a consequence of these attempts to promote discontent through the press; and that the proceedings of abolitionists generally having greatly exasperated the slaveholders, the condition of slaves was now very much worse than if there had been no abolition movement. There is perhaps some truth, but also some error, in these statements.*

It may, we think, be candidly admitted, that the ultra-abolitionists—like the old English Puritans and the Scotch Covenanters—take extreme views of the subject, are rather intractable, and, from conscientious but not extensively appreciated motives, do not scruple to denounce what they consider to be a great national sin. Thus, they give offence. Their language is occasionally coarse and irreverent. For example, one of Garrison's common expressions is, that 'the United States constitution is a Covenant with Death, and an

---

* According to the *Baltimore American*, slaves are now much better treated than formerly: 'Though abolitionists may disguise the fact, the general current of legislation at the South for years past has been in favour of the slave. His rights have been more looked after, his person better protected; and when these ends have not been sought by positive enactment, the gradual but firm influence of the moral sentiment of the people has tended practically to the most beneficial amelioration of his condition.' If this be correct, what becomes of the charge that the proceedings of abolitionists have greatly aggravated the hardships of the slaves?

Agreement with Hell'—an abuse of Scriptural phraseology not exactly accordant with modern notions. It may be also allowed that the anti-slavery cause has been sullied by unseemly party differences, and that, assuming the worst qualities of sectarians, its adherents have too often demonstrated a spirit of intolerance and persecution.

Until very lately, we were disposed to think that no abolitionists had gone the length of recommending insurrection as a means of abolition; and still it would be hard to fix the charge of doing so on the whole party which should in justice apply only to a few of the less prudent members. We here allude to certain propositions of Frederick Douglass, in his newspaper for November 28, 1856, in which he appears to contend for the right and duty of revolt.* Garrison, on the other hand, who is in many respects a remarkable man —bold, independent, and indefatigable—has, we believe, always disclaimed an appeal to physical violence, and by the force of his character has stamped a pacific policy on the movement with which he is associated.

Whatever may have been the opinions entertained

---

* 'While we feel bound to use all our powers of persuasion and argument; to welcome every instrumentality that promises to peacefully destroy that perpetual contemner of God's laws, and disturber of a nation's peace—Slavery; we yet feel that its peaceful annihilation is almost hopeless, and hence stand by the doctrines enunciated in those resolutions, and contend that the slave's right to revolt is perfect, and only wants the occurrence of favourable circumstances to become a duty. . . . . We cannot but shudder as we call to mind the horrors that have ever marked servile insurrections—we would avert them if we could; but shall the millions for ever submit to robbery, to murder, to ignorance, and every unnamed evil which an irresponsible tyranny can devise, because the overthrow of that tyranny would be productive of horrors? We say not. The recoil, when it comes, will be in exact proportion to the wrongs inflicted; terrible as it will be, we accept and hope for it. The slaveholder has been tried and sentenced, his execution only waits the finish to the training of his executioners. He is training his own executioners.'

respecting abolitionist doctrines, the time has come when they must be spoken of at least in terms of extenuation. The occurrences of the last twelve months have immeasurably advanced the anti-slavery cause in the minds of Europeans; and we may add, that on the relative situation of abolitionists and slaveholders a new and more distinct light has been thrown. The recent declaration by leading organs in the South, that slavery was there and there for ever—that no plan of emancipation would be listened to—that slavery is a natural and proper institution—that free society has been a failure—that the whole free coloured and poor white population of the States should be reduced to perpetual bondage—that the foreign slave trade ought to be revived—together with eulogies on slavery by the Governors of a state, and also by a President of the United States—declarations by the highest authorities that there is an inherent vitality in slavery which will insure its illimitable growth; and a distinct avowal of the design to absorb new countries for the sake of protecting and greatly extending the institution—these extraordinary announcements, along with the unprovoked and unredressed outrages committed by Missourians in Kansas, the brutal assault of Brooks on Mr Sumner, not to speak of other barbarities, defended and gloried in—all this, we say, entirely alters the aspect under which we are to view the operations of the abolitionists. As long as the world was under the impression that a calm consideration of emancipation was postponed in consequence of the intemperate harangues of what were deemed a body of fanatics, the slaveholders commanded that degree of sympathy which was thought to be due to their undesired and very unfortunate situation. But now, with the facts before us, we are at a loss to see how the matter is to be treated in the same indulgent spirit,

Lamenting the past rudeness with which abolitionists have pressed their opinions—believing they would have more successfully promoted their aims by using milder persuasives—persons of enlarged views will join us in looking beyond the Faneuil Hall and Exeter Hall aspect of the anti-slavery cause. This cause is not to be regarded merely as it affects the blacks, but the whites—not merely the South, but the North—not merely the United States, but the whole family of mankind. All the communities on earth are interested in the solution of this mighty question—which, like other social questions of any consequence, has had to pass primarily through the hands of agitators who care little for conventional respectabilities. The question, we apprehend, has now got beyond the narrow sphere of anti-slavery societies. Supposing, that the whole of the associations were dissolved and done with, that no such men as Garrison, Wendell Phillips, or Sumner were in existence, we return to general principles, and hope it will not be thought intrusive, if we ask the American people to be so good as explain, *what they propose to do with four millions of negro slaves and their progeny?*

Abolition principles are said to be making progress in the North. The protracted struggle in Kansas affords evidence of a desire somewhere, to outflank slavery on its own ground. Still, there is a universal disinclination to meddle with southern institutions. If we admit that an important end is gained by excluding slavery from Kansas, is there not the great south and south-west at disposal? From Texas and New Mexico, a number of new slave states may be carved out. We are aware that by the more sanguine class of American writers, it is confidently believed that Mexico, peopled as it is by mixed breeds hostile to American usages, will form an impregnable barrier to slavery in the south-west. How like one of the delusive fancies ordinarily indulged on the subject! With power in the hands of the pro-slavery party, and under a pressure for labour, the absorption of Mexico, Central America, and Cuba is only a question of time and expediency. The very mixture of breeds in Mexico invites aggression. In the growing scarcity and costliness of negroes, there lies in that doomed country ample material at hand, ready for seizure and inter-state deportation. For anything the present generation can tell, the South, Mexico included, may, some hundreds of years hence, form a great free republic of blacks, the refuge of oppressed colour. Such, indeed, is likely to be the case; but before that era comes round, what suffering, what convulsions, what bloodshed!

Slavery, we repeat, is seemingly destined to push far beyond its present limits. Is no check practicable?

The Constitution—it can do nothing.

The Republicans—they possess little political power; and besides, they propose to act solely through the constitution.

The North—the majority of its representatives faithless; confidence in politicians gone.

The Anti-slavery Societies—a scattered body, with unfashionable views, and no political weight.

Enlightened Opinion—suppressed by mob violence and outvoted; the less opulent and more numerous classes being democrats, and supporters of the slave power.

The South—resolute in maintaining its institutions, and master of the situation.

Patience: the next decennial census will add to the number of members in congress from the free states; the free states will be increased in number by Minnesota, Nebraska, Oregon, and Washington—perhaps so much the worse; more democratic votes, more political manœuvring, more slavery?

There exists a hope of modifying slavery, by a diversion of the cotton trade from America, and by a removal of protective duties. A falling off in the demand for American cotton, by lessening the demand for negroes, would affect the slave-breeding states, and dispose them to adopt freedom. By the removal of protection, the present compact between North and South would be greatly shaken. The former point is for the consideration of Englishmen; the latter for that of Americans.

There is another hope to which we may call attention. It is the possibility of creating a free state in Western Texas, by means of the German and other European immigrants who have settled in that slave section of the Union. Whether the Free-soilers may here be able to outflank slavery, is doubtful; but the attempt will be made, and the people of England need not be surprised to learn that the outrages by slaveholders in Kansas are re-enacted on a scale of greater desperation near the shores of the Gulf of Mexico.

We would not willingly resign our faith in the capacity of Americans for overcoming dangers and difficulties. They possess a wonderful power of rallying when things are at their worst. Some grand movement, inspired by virtuous indignation and despair, may dislodge the oligarchy which controls public policy on the slave question. New Washingtons, Franklins, and Quincey Adamses may arise, to sustain the cause of freedom, now basely pronounced to be a failure. It is consoling to know that sudden and unforeseen changes for the better take place in the social as in the physical atmosphere. Luther's reformation was precipitated by the sale of some paltry indulgences. The fear of abolitionism, which now, like a superstition, hangs over the United States, preventing the dispassionate consideration of a subject of momentous concern, may, from some unforeseen cause, be speedily and happily dispelled.

Looking at matters as they stand, however, making every allowance for contingencies, we sorrowfully admit that these events do not seem probable. To be quite plain: there appear—at least on the surface—to be but two expedients, by which this fearfully embarrassed question is to be solved—Revolution, Insurrection, both to be earnestly deprecated.

Lately, apart from the old-school abolitionists, there have sprung up societies in Massachusetts and other quarters, with the distinctly professed object of dissolving the Union; in order that the free states may no longer be associated with, or made responsible for slave institutions. Which states are to be disunited, these societies do not mention; that apparently being left to chance. They expect to operate through petitions to congress—hopeless. The law, unchangeable by peaceful means, is against them; and with the universally prevailing respect for the Union, which with Americans is a kind of sub-religion, we do not imagine that the doctrines of the Disunionists will meet with wider acceptance than those of the Abolitionists, of which they are only a new version.*

By writers who have taken notice of this new movement, Disunion is disapproved of, on the ground that if effected, slavery would be maintained with greater vigour in the South; they even speculate on the probability of some millions of abject whites in the southern states being made slaves. We think differently. The withdrawal of the northern states from the confederacy, whether peacefully or by armed force, would so shake and weaken the whole fabric of southern institutions,

---

* For Resolutions proposed at a Disunion Convention at Worcester, Massachusetts, see Appendix.

that an insurrection by the slaves would be inevitable—slavery would dissolve in a sea of blood.

The South knows this. It has often, in its vaunting and reckless mode of speaking, threatened to quit the Union. Let it try.*

Feeling its power, the North, if true to itself and animated by higher motives, could in a short space of time extinguish slavery. It could say to the South: 'Unless you proceed to follow our example, and make provision for the gradual emancipation of your slaves, the partnership between us must be dissolved; we must quit the confederacy, and be to you in future a foreign country.' A resolute but friendly address in these terms from an aggregate convention of free states is what civilisation would point to, instead of a resort to arms. But what a glow of patriotism—what an arousing of sensibilities—what a casting forth of selfishness—what a disruption of venerated traditions—what an enlightening of the masses—must ensue before the North assumes this grand attitude! It will not do so. The execution of the threat would be Revolution.

A declaration of independence by Massachusetts, or any other single state, is equally, if not more improbable; for that would be equivalent to civil war—an issue not likely to be contemplated. We would not, however, say with any certainty, that Massachusetts

* Mr T. D. Arnold of Tennessee, in a speech in the House of Representatives, stated the case correctly: 'He would ask his southern friends what the South had to rely on if the Union were dissolved? Suppose the dissolution could be peaceably effected—if that did not involve a contradiction in terms—what had the South to depend upon? *All the crowned heads were against her. A million of slaves were ready to rise and strike for freedom at the first tap of the drum.* They were cut loose from their friends at the North—friends that ought to be, and without them the South had no friends—*whither were they to look for protection?* How were they to sustain an assault from England or France, with that cancer at their vitals? The more the South reflected, the more clearly she must see that she had a deep and vital interest in maintaining the Union.'

would tamely submit to a *very* lengthened repetition of the indignities to which it has latterly been subjected by federal agencies. Spectators at a distance wait with some interest to see which is to be the last outrage that is to revive the spirit of Bunker's Hill.

The consideration of pacific adjustment being deliberately rejected, and Disunion, Revolution, or Civil War abjured—the case is not mended. Slavery goes on uninterruptedly in its course. The sore spreads, festers, and the longer a corrective is delayed, the disease becomes worse, the danger more imminent.

One trembles at the fatal alternative: Revolution—Insurrection. Can insurrection be avoided either way? Revolution would produce insurrection. Successful insurrection would be followed by revolution; for we can scarcely expect that the North would remain in union with a nation of blacks. Were the South to secede in a paroxysm of indignation in the appointment of a Republican president, in 1860, we do not see how the chance of immediate or ultimate conflict between slavery and freedom would be lessened; it would, in all probability, be precipitated.

But while the whole federal power may be brought to suppress revolt, how can the slaves be successful in insurrection? War with one of the great European powers would furnish the means at once! God forbid that we should advocate such a crisis; but the history we have been tracing leads the mind, however reluctantly, to such a possibility; and it is impossible to avoid seeing that events are within the range even of probability which would render insurrection, if it occurred, not only formidable, but successful. If these pages awaken, before it is too late, some of the more powerful minds of America to the catastrophe to which, in the eyes of dispassionate observers, the history of their country seems tending, I shall not have written in vain.

POSTSCRIPT.

Since the foregoing was written, events have occurred which are likely to lead to a settlement of the slave question more speedily than could have been anticipated. Since 1856, certain free states, to the number of fifteen, have enacted statutes calculated to defeat the operation of the federal Fugitive Slave Law; by which the northern states practically become a refuge for the runaway 'property' of the South. Irritated on this score, the slave-holding states, or, more properly, those in which cotton is the staple product, rose to a climax of indignation on the appointment as President of Abraham Lincoln, a member of the Republican party, in 1860 (inauguration, March 4, 1861)—one of the expected results of the installation of this free-soiler being, that a check would be put to the further extension of slavery in the Territories.

The immediate consequence of the successful nomination of Lincoln, was the formal, though perhaps not constitutional, secession of South Carolina from the Union, December 20, 1860. Unchecked, if not aided by Mr Buchanan, the secession movement spread to other southern states; and now, June 1861, there are at least ten seceding states in open rebellion. It is to be feared that this most unhappy civil war, if not promptly quelled, will lead to an abrupt servile insurrection, and that form of solution of the slave question above hinted at. On a supposition, however, even of an amicable adjustment of the matters in dispute, the Americans will no longer be able to treat the subject of slavery with reserve; so that, any way, the cause of freedom cannot fail to be materially advanced.

APPENDIX.

ILLUSTRATIVE SCRAPS FROM VARIOUS SOURCES.

GUILT OF GREAT BRITAIN IN INTRODUCING SLAVERY.

SINCE writing the early chapters of the present volume, my attention has been called to a work, entitled *Who is to Blame?* by James Grahame, Esq., author of a History of the United States (London: Smith and Elder, 1842). Mr Grahame's object is to shew that British traders only offered facilities to the colonists for purchasing slaves; that the proprietary colonies adopted slavery, and strenuously supported it of their own accord; and that the English government had little or nothing to do with planting slavery in America. We recommend Mr Grahame's scholarly and temperately written work to the perusal of those who feel interested in this historical question.

Referring to a panegyric on slavery by Governor Miller of South Carolina, as early as 1829, Mr Grahame observes:

'While America was subject to British domination, no magistrate of an American state ever gave the sanction of magisterial authority to such sentiments as these; and no pulpit was ever profaned with the apologies for slavery which the clergymen of republican America are now not ashamed to preach. Jonathan Edwards, the most admirable teacher of Christian doctrine and pattern of Christian character that America, or perhaps the world, has produced since the apostolic age, during the ascendancy of Britain, denounced the system of slavery, and urged its *immediate* abolition by his countrymen, with a boldness and security of unreproved freedom to which the present race of Americans are utter strangers. And was it then to make America a theatre for such disgraceful display as we have witnessed, that the pious Puritans undertook their pilgrimage to New England—that the peaceful Quakers retired to Pennsylvania—that Catholics flying from persecution in Britain, set to the world the first example of religious toleration in Maryland—that La Fayette and Kosciusko shed their blood in the cause of American Independence—and that Washington, Franklin, Adams, Jefferson, Jay, and Henry, made for themselves and their country a glorious and immortal name? Every one of these men entertained and expressed a strong abhorrence of negro slavery. If, by fatal necessity, America *must* copy, in her civil policy, the vices as well as the virtues of Greece and Rome—if the lawless abuse must always be proportioned to the legitimate enjoyment of freedom—then is America fated to afford the most humiliating illustration ever witnessed by the world, of Milton's melancholy sentiment:

> "Since the original lapse, *true liberty*
> *Is lost*, which always with right reason dwells
> Twinn'd, and from her hath no dividual being."'

POPULATION OF THE UNITED STATES ACCORDING TO THE SEVENTH CENSUS, AND REPRESENTATIVES IN CONGRESS.*

States.	White Population.	Free Coloured Population.	Total Free.	Slaves.	Federal Representative Population.	No. of Representatives.	Gain or Loss from last Cen.	Fractions over.
Maine,	581,813	1,356	583,169		583,169	6	—1	22,631
New Hampshire,	317,436	526	317,976		317,976	3	—1	37,707
Vermont,	313,402	718	314,120		314,120	3	—1	33,851
Massachusetts,	985,450	9,064	994,514		994,514	11	+1	60,284
Rhode Island,	143,875	3,670	147,545		147,545	2		54,122
Connecticut,	363,099	7,693	370,792		370,792	4		90,523
New York,	3,048,325	49,069	3,097,391		3,097,394	33	—3	14,433
New Jersey,	408,512	23,820	489,333	222	489,400	5		22,351
Pennsylvania,	2,258,403	53,328	2,311,786		2,311,786	25	+1	69,634
Delaware,	71,169	18,073	89,242	2,290	90,616	1		
Maryland,	417,943	74,723	492,666	90,368	540,856	6		79,771
Virginia,	894,800	54,333	949,133	472,528	1,232,649	13	—2	18,150
North Carolina,	553,026	27,463	580,491	288,548	753,619	8	—1	6,223
South " ,	274,567	8,956	283,523	384,984	514,513	6	—1	447,398
Georgia,	521,572	2,931	524,503	381,682	753,512	8		6,129
Florida,	47,211	928	48,133	39,309	71,720	1		
Alabama,	426,486	2,293	428,779	342,892	634,514	7		73,976
Mississippi,	295,718	930	296,648	309,878	482,571	5	+1	15,496
Louisiana,	255,491	17,462	272,953	244,800	410,838	4		40,140
Texas,	154,034	397	154,431	58,101	189,327	2		2,481
Arkansas,	162,189	608	162,797	47,100	191,037	2	+1	4,211
Tennessee,	756,753	6,401	763,154	239,460	906,836	10	—1	66,023
Kentucky,	761,417	10,007	771,421	210,981	898,012	10		457,203
Missouri,	592,004	2,618	594,622	87,422	647,076	7	+2	86,537
Ohio,	1,955,108	25,319	1,980,427		1,980,427	21		18,544
Michigan,	395,007	2,587	397,654		307,654	4	+1	23,062
Indiana,	977,025	10,788	988,416		988,416	11	+1	54,180
Illinois,	846,033	5,485	851,470		851,470	9	+2	10,006
Wisconsin,	304,758	633	305,391		305,391	3		25,123
Iowa,	191,873	333	192,214		192,214	2		5,368
California,	91,632	965	92,597		92,597	2		
Total,	19,423,013	423,384	19,847,301	3,200,634	21,767,673	234		
Dist. of Columbia,	38,027	9,973	48,000	3,687				
Minnesota,	6,038	39	6,077					
New Mexico,	61,530	17	61,547					
Oregon,	13,088	203	13,204					
Utah,	11,330	24	11,354	26				
Total,	19,533,926	433,642	19,967,573	3,204,347				

RECAPITULATION.

	Total Population in 1840.	Slaves in 1840.	Total Population in 1850.	Total Free Population in 1850.	Slaves in 1850.	Representative Pop. in 1850.	Rep. in 1850.	Gain or Loss.
Free States,	9,654,865	1,102	13,434,922	13,434,798		13,430,931	144	+1
Slave States,	7,290,719	2,481,532	9,612,969	6,412,563	3,200,412	8,330,742	90	—1
Dist. and Ter.	117,769	4,721	142,965	140,272	3,713			
Total,	17,063,353	2,487,355	23,191,876	19,987,573	3,204,347	21,767,673	234	

* The aggregate representative population (21,767,673), divided by 233—the number of representatives established by law—gives 93,425 as the ratio of apportionment among the several States. But this gives only 220 members, leaving 13 to be assigned to the States having the largest residuary fractions.

† In the column of fractions, those marked thus,†, entitle the State to an additional Representative, who is included in the number given the State in the column of Representatives.

‡ By the act of July 30, 1852, an additional representative is assigned to California, making the whole number of Representatives 234. The ratio of representation remains unchanged. The last published census tables differ slightly from the above, but as the apportionment of representation is made by above table, it is continued.

POPULATION OF THE UNITED STATES.

States.	1790.	1800.	1810.	1820.	1830.	1840.	1850.
Maine,	96,540	151,719	228,705	298,335	399,955	501,793	583,169
N. Hampshire	141,899	183,762	214,360	244,161	269,328	284,574	317,976
Vermont,	85,416	154,465	217,713	235,764	280,652	291,948	314,120
Massachusetts	378,717	422,245	472,040	523,287	610,408	737,699	994,514
Rhode Island,	69,110	69,122	77,031	83,059	97,199	108,830	147,545
Connecticut,	238,141	251,002	262,042	275,202	297,665	309,978	370,792
New York,	340,120	586,756	959,949	1,372,812	1,918,608	2,428,921	3,097,304
" Jersey	184,139	211,949	249,555	277,575	320,823	373,306	489,555
Pennsylvania,	434,373	602,365	810,091	1,049,458	1,318,233	1,724,033	2,811,786
Delaware,	59,096	64,273	72,674	72,749	76,748	78,086	91,532
Maryland,	319,728	341,548	380,546	407,350	447,040	470,019	583,034
Virginia,	748,305	880,200	974,612	1,065,379	1,211,405	1,239,797	1,421,661
N. Carolina,	393,751	478,103	555,500	638,629	737,987	753,419	869,039
S. "	249,073	345,591	415,715	502,741	581,185	594,398	668,507
Georgia,	82,548	162,101	252,433	340,987	516,823	691,592	906,185
Florida,					34,730	54,477	87,415
Alabama,			20,845	127,901	309,527	590,756	771,623
Mississippi,		8,850	40,352	75,448	136,621	375,651	606,526
Louisiana,			76,556	153,407	215,739	352,411	517,762
Texas,							212,592
Arkansas,				14,272	30,338	97,574	209,897
Tennessee,	30,791	105,002	261,727	422,813	681,904	829,210	1,002,717
Kentucky,	73,077	220,955	406,511	564,317	687,917	779,828	982,405
Ohio,		45,365	230,760	581,434	937,503	1,519,467	1,980,329
Michigan,			4,762	8,896	31,639	212,267	397,654
Indiana,		4,875	24,520	147,178	343,031	685,866	988,416
Illinois,			12,282	55,211	157,435	476,183	851,470
Missouri,			20,845	66,586	140,445	383,702	682,014
Wisconsin,						30,943	305,391
Iowa,						43,112	192,214
Dis. of Colum.		14,093	24,023	33,039	39,834	43,712	51,687
California,							92,597
Total,	3,929,872	5,305,952	7,239,814	9,638,131	12,866,920	17,063,353	23,191,876

SLAVES IN THE UNITED STATES.

States.	1790.	1800.	1810.	1820.	1830.	1840.	1850.
Maine,	0	0	0	0	0	0	0
N. Hampshire	158	8	0	0	0	1	0
Vermont,	17	0	0	0	0	0	0
Massachusetts	0	0	0	0	0	0	0
Rhode Island,	952	381	103	48	17	5	0
Connecticut,	2,750	951	310	97	25	17	0
New York,	21,324	20,343	15,017	10,088	75	4	0
" Jersey,	11,423	12,422	10,851	7,657	2,254	674	286
Pennsylvania,	3,737	1,706	795	211	403	61	0
Delaware,	8,887	6,153	4,177	4,509	3,292	2,605	2,290
Maryland,	103,036	105,635	111,502	107,805	102,294	89,737	90,368
Virginia,	293,427	345,796	392,518	425,153	469,757	448,987	472,528
N. Carolina,	100,572	133,296	168,824	295,017	235,601	245,817	288,548
S. "	107,094	146,151	196,865	258,475	315,401	327,038	384,984
Florida,					15,501	25,717	39,310
Georgia,	29,264	59,404	105,218	149,656	217,531	280,944	381,682
Alabama,				41,879	117,549	253,532	342,844
Mississippi,		3,430	17,088	32,814	65,650	195,211	309,878
Louisiana,			34,660	69,064	109,588	166,452	244,800
Texas,							58,161
Arkansas,				1,617	4,576	19,935	47,100
Tennessee,	3,417	13,584	44,535	80,107	141,603	183,059	239,459
Kentucky,	11,830	40,343	80,561	126,732	165,213	182,258	210,981
Ohio,					0	3	0
Michigan,			24		32	0	0
Indiana,		135	237	190	6	3	0
Illinois,			168	117	747	331	0
Missouri,			3,011	10,222	25,081	58,240	87,422
Wisconsin,						11	0
Iowa,						16	0
California,							0
Dis. of Colum.		3,244	5,395	6,377	6,119	4,694	3,687
Total,	697,897	893,041	1,191,364	1,538,064	2,009,031	2,487,355	3,204,313

PROGRESSIVE INCREASE OF POPULATION.

Comparative population of the United States in 1800, 1850, and 1900—adding 3 per cent. per annum, the ascertained increase from 1800 to 1850, to the latter period:

	Total in 1800.	Total in 1850.	Estimated in 1900.
Free States,	2,684,625	13,527,300	62,000,000
Slave States,	2,621,300	9,664,576	36,000,000
Total estimate of Population in 1900,			98,000,000

Of which, by ascertained ratio of increase, the slave population will be 12,000,000, leaving 86,000,000 freemen in the year 1900, of which only 24,000,000 will be in the southern states.

Estimated increase from 1850 to 1900, in periods of ten years, adding 3 per cent. per annum:

			Total Pop.	Slaves.
Total population in 1850,			23,191,870	3,204,813
" " " 1860,			31,095,535	4,157,787
" " " 1870,			40,617,708	5,465,173
" " " 1880,			54,586,795	7,026,659
" " " 1890,			73,332,185	9,134,656
" " " 1900,			98,595,512	11,875,000

Long before this latter period arrives, it is to be hoped that slavery will have ceased to exist in these United States, and that the census of this modern republic will not be disgraced by a display of freemen and bondmen side by side, as at present appears in fifteen out of thirty-one of the States of the Union.—*American Newspaper.*

DANGEROUS CONDITION OF COLOURED PERSONS.

It has been stated that free persons of colour from the northern states are in danger of lapsing into slavery, by merely intruding within the verge of a slave state. In Maryland, there was a law passed in 1839, to prohibit the ingress of free persons of colour, under the penalty of a heavy fine. The enactment is as follows: 'No free negro or mulatto, belonging to, or residing in any other state, is permitted to come into Maryland, whether such free negro or mulatto intends settling in this state or not, under the penalty of 20 dollars for the first offence.' For a second offence, the penalty is 500 dollars; and, failing the payment of such fines, the offender 'shall be committed to the jail of the county, and shall be sold by the sheriff at public sale to the highest bidder.'

Under this law, a free coloured person wandering inadvertently into Maryland in quest of employment, may be seized, and if poor and unable to pay the fine, sold after a few days' public notice, just as if he were a stray heifer. A case of this kind occurred not long ago.

In 1851, there resided in Philadelphia a negro named Edward Davis, who, finding employment fail, went to the country in quest of the means of subsistence. He could not have possessed very bright intelligence, for he ought to have known that it was dangerous for him to enter the borders of a slave state. His original intention was to go no further than Hollidaysburgh, a flourishing town in Blair county, Pennsylvania; but for some reason he abandoned this design, and crossing the Susquehanna, reached the populous village of Havre de Grace, in Maryland. Here he sought for, and obtained employment; and was thoughtlessly pursuing his occupation, when he was arrested, and taken before a magistrate, to answer the charge of having violated the law, which prohibits the settlement of free negroes in the state. The offence was clear, and the fine of twenty dollars incurred. Destitute of money, and without friends, he was confined in prison, where he lay about two months. At the end of this period, he was brought out, and after due advertisement, sold by auction to pay his fine and expenses—altogether amounting to fifty dollars. The following is a copy of the sheriff's certificate of sale, which we give as a curiosity:

'State of Maryland, Harford county—I, Robert M'Gan, sheriff of Harford county, do hereby certify, that whereas negro Ned Davis was found guilty by the Orphan Court of Harford county of a violation of the Act of Assembly of the state of Maryland, passed 1839, chapter 38; and the said negro having refused to pay the fine and costs, as in the said law directed, I did, having first given the notice prescribed by law, expose the said negro at public sale, at the court-house doors in Bell Air, and Dr John G. Archer, of Louisiana, being the highest bidder, became the purchaser of the said negro. Given under my hand and seal, this tenth day of November 1851. Robert M'Gan, sheriff.'

Davis, now a slave, was subsequently transferred from master to master; and we find that, in June 1852, he was sold to a Mr Dean of Macon, Georgia, for 300 dollars. As this is only about a third of the market-value of an able-bodied negro, we infer that he was past the prime of life, or otherwise defective. In one of the accounts of the transaction, he is spoken of as being thirty-four years of age. Be this as it may, Ned Davis was, to all intents and purposes, a slave; and as such, was first employed to cook for a large number of slaves in Baltimore; and subsequently, on being purchased by Mr Dean, was sent southward, through Washington and Charleston, to Georgia. On arriving in Macon, he was put to work on a railway; but the labour of an excavator being beyond his strength, his health failed, and, as a relief, he was placed on a cotton-plantation. He was afterwards sent back to the railway. This second time, however, he utterly broke down, and was removed to an hospital. This occurred in July 1853. In the hospital, he related his history to the attending physicians, who, taking pity on him, offered to buy him for 400 dollars; but the price was refused. Although shattered in health, and partially lame, the unfortunate Ned was again put to some kind of work, and he continued in servitude till the 12th of March 1854. On this day, after long brooding over his wrongs, he ran away from Macon, and went to Savannah, a seaport from which steam-vessels traded to northern free states. Davis's object was to get on board one of these vessels; and he secreted himself in a stable till the 14th, on which day he went on board the steamer *Keystone State*, which was to sail next morning for Philadelphia. The remainder of the narrative may be given in the words of a New York newspaper:

'At nine o'clock the next morning, the steamer sailed with Davis on board. The following day, the men, while heaving the lead, heard a voice from under the guards of the boat, calling for them to throw him a rope. Upon examination, it was found that the voice proceeded from a coloured man, concealed on a beam under the guards of the wheel-house. He was rescued from his perilous situation, in a state of great exhaustion: his clothes were saturated with sea-water, as the sea had become rough, and he was dipped in the water at every rock of the vessel. The hands furnished him with a dry suit, and made him comfortable; but the commander of the boat was differently disposed. Fearing the effects of Georgian law, in case he should bring a slave to a free state, he ordered his vessel to put into Newcastle, Delaware, where he had the unfortunate man imprisoned, with the intention, it is stated, of taking him back to Savannah on his return-trip. But the facts of the case having leaked out, public sympathy was enlisted, and a determination shewn that Davis should not go back to Georgia, unless it could be established that he was not entitled to his freedom. On the 20th of March, the case was brought before Justice Bradford, of Newcastle. A number of witnesses were examined, and his freedom clearly proved. On hearing this testimony in his favour, the magistrate discharged him from custody, there being no reason why a free citizen of Pennsylvania should be kept in a Delaware prison, with no crime charged against him. After his discharge, and before he had left the magistrate's office, the commander of the *Keystone State* appeared; made affidavit that he believed Davis to be a fugitive slave, and also a fugitive from justice; whereupon he was detained, and again shut up in prison.' On the return of the captain of the steamer to Savannah, measures were adopted to reclaim possession of Davis by legal proceedings. The case came on for trial at Newcastle, April 16; and it was clearly proved by evidence, that the negro had been legally seized and sold in Maryland, and transferred by his owners to his present claimant, Mr Dean. A decision was given accordingly; the runaway being adjudged to be a slave, and put at the disposal of his proprietor. Whether he was actually taken back to Georgia, is not stated. If alive, there can be no doubt of his being still in a condition of slavery. The laws of Pennsylvania possess no power to reclaim a citizen, whose liberty is legally forfeited in another state; and if the friends of Ned Davis fail to buy him, there are, so far as we are aware, no other lawful means by which they can restore him to freedom.

AMALGAMATION.

There was published in London, in 1853, a small volume, entitled *The American Prejudice against Colour; an Authentic Narrative.* By Willam G. Allen.* Allen's narrative is curious. He tells us that he is a quadroon, one-fourth African blood, and three-fourths Anglo-Saxon. He received a good education, and graduated at Oneida Institute, in Whitesboro, state of New York, in 1844. Subsequently, he studied law, and became professor of the Greek and German languages, and of rhetoric and belles-lettres, of New York Central College, in M'Grawville, Cortland county—the only college in America that has ever called a coloured man to a professorship. In

* W. and F. G. Cash, Bishopsgate Street. Price One Shilling.

April 1851, he visited Fulton to deliver a course of lectures. Here he was kindly received by the Rev. Lyndon King, a Wesleyan Methodist clergyman, to one of whose daughters, Miss Mary King, he ultimately became attached. The sentiment was reciprocal. The father of the young lady had no objection to his offer of marriage; one of the young lady's sisters, also, favoured the proposal; but Mrs King—a step-mother—and the other members of the family, were violently opposed to the idea of forming a connection with a man of colour. The greatest opponent of all was one of the brothers, the Rev. J. B. King, a prodigiously pious gentleman, who had for some time been engaged in gathering funds to build a church, which should exclude from membership those who held their fellow-men in bondage, and all who would not admit the doctrines of the human brotherhood! Professing an abhorrence of slavery, he nevertheless seems to have possessed the usual northern prejudice against persons of colour. He was incensed beyond measure at the atrocity of the proposed alliance; and through him and the stepmother the public indignation appears to have been excited. From less to more, all Fulton and its neighbourhood were roused to a sense of the impropriety of the intended marriage—the objections resting on no other grounds than the damage that might be done to the pure Anglo-Saxon race by *amalgamation* with the African type.

Professor Allen and Miss King were now placed in an awkward and dangerous predicament. Besides the lady's sister, their only friend was Mr Porter, a schoolmaster, and his wife. Porter allowed the parties to meet at his house. Having gone thither on Sunday evening, January 30, 1853, for the purpose of talking over their affairs, they were alarmed by the intelligence that an infuriated mob was collecting, which would soon surround the house, and commit some serious personal outrage. Allen was informed that 'tar, feathers, poles, and an empty barrel, spiked with shingle nails, had been prepared for his especial benefit;' Mr Porter was to be tarand-feathered, and ridden on a rail; and Miss King was to be conducted away in a sleigh to the house of her parents. Aware of the extremities to which the mob-spirit is carried on such occasions, Allen prepared for death. Unless the mob relented, no earthly power could save him.

Up the outrageous multitude at length came. They consisted of all classes of persons, including the most respectable in the place. The churches were emptied; all went off to enjoy the fun or mischief of hunting 'the nigger,' and protesting against the sin of amalgamation. With shouts and yells, the mob called to 'bring out the nigger,' 'to kill him,' and 'to tear down the house.' Some members of a committee who had been appointed to regulate proceedings, entered the dwelling, and declared that Allen's life could only be saved by his instant departure, and that Miss King would at the same time require to go home to her parents. The young lady having, after some demur, gone off in a sleigh, Allen was next escorted from the house by the members of committee to a hotel—not, however, without being well kicked and buffeted by the mob, who crowded about him during the march. At the hotel, after a little delay, he was smuggled away by a back-entrance, and conveyed in a sleigh to Syracuse—a distance of about twenty-five miles.

Dark days ensued. The newspapers were furious at the idea of amalgamation, and it was some time before the lovers were able to arrange an interview. We must refer to Allen's narrative for an account of what indignities were suffered by both parties at this period. Some time in March, they were enabled to see each other, and to arrange future movements. At this interview they resolved to exercise their undoubted legal rights—to enter into the holy state of matrimony; but having done so, to flee the country. This daring resolution they successfully put into effect. They were married in New York, and shortly afterwards departed from Boston for Liverpool. Professor Allen carried recommendations with him to gentlemen in England, by whom he has probably been put in the way of earning a livelihood. He, in conclusion, informs his readers, that Mr Porter, who gave him refuge in adversity, was dismissed from his situation as schoolmaster, in consequence of outraging public opinion by favouring the union of a white lady with a man degraded by the taint of African blood. If all this be true—and we have no reason to doubt its authenticity—we are furnished with a striking example of that loathing and detestation of the free coloured population which prevails in the northern states of the Union, and which has seemed to us so irreconcilable with the profession of anti-slavery principles.

TEACHING FREE COLOURED CHILDREN TO READ.

'Slavery not only precludes education by its very nature—it enacts laws *to secure ignorance* among the *free citizens* of the slave states. By the laws of Virginia, Mrs Douglass, of Norfolk, was pronounced guilty of a "crime" for teaching *free* coloured children to read. She suffered thirty days' imprisonment in the city jail, not because it is actually a *crime* to teach a free coloured child to read, but because intelligence is dangerous to slavery. It was necessary to make an example of her, to deter all future offenders. Judge Baker has won an unenviable notoriety in his delivery of her sentence. He says that the idea that universal culture is necessary to religious instruction and education is "mischievous"—a well-chosen term. He says that of all the negroes in the world, none are so intelligent, so inclined to the Gospel, and so blessed by the elevating influences of the Gospel, as the slaves of the United States, and that if any one would have their interests more carefully regarded than they are by the laws of Virginia, it must be from a sickly sensibility towards them. Then he proceeds to vindicate the justice of the sentence by the fact that, "*in good sense and sound morality*, his discretionary power to imprison for six months or less does not authorise a mere minimum punishment," since the question of "*guilt*" is beyond a doubt; and there are many "aggravating circumstances." "Therefore, as a terror to those who acknowledge no rule of action but their own *evil* will and pleasure, and in vindication of the *justness* of our laws, the judgment of the court is, that you be imprisoned for the period of one month in the jail of this city." Because Mrs Douglass chose to remain and suffer the full penalty of the law, though all the citizens hoped she would leave the city, the *Norfolk Argus* of February 9, 1854, says: "Then sympathy departed, and in the breast of every one rose a *righteous* indignation towards a person who would throw *contempt* in the face of the laws, and brave the imprisonment for the 'cause of humanity.'"'—*Tract: Influence of Slavery upon the White Population.*

SLAVERY, A DOMESTIC INSTITUTION.

'By a strange misnomer, slavery has been called a "domestic" institution; but before its presence all that is properly implied in that word *domestic* vanishes like an exorcised spirit. The desolation wrought among the coloured victims of slavery is terrible, and mighty indeed is their demand for redress; but they have their revenge in the wreck of the domestic happiness of their oppressors.

'I have said that the white child is committed entirely to the care of the coloured nurse, and thus the process of contamination begins in infancy. Young children are familiarised to sights and associations which destroy the instinctive modesty of youth. They are also placed in such relations to the coloured children, through the ignorance or malice of the nurse, as to stimulate the passions into premature activity. Some nurses believe that personal intimacies between the young master and his young female companions cultivate a closer affection, and insure the latter from the chances of being sold. Others, of a fiercer temper, seek their revenge for outrages committed on themselves, in order to exult over the wreck of early manhood always resulting from self-indulgence. By whichever process the result is attained, it is a well-known fact that purity among southern men is almost an unknown virtue.

'There are thousands of proofs of this in the prevalence of the fair skin, smooth and glossy hair, blue eyes, straight nose, delicate foot, and arched instep, which are everywhere to be met among the slaves. But why should we expect purity when every restraint is removed which helps to subdue the clamours of the animal nature, while every possible opportunity is offered for its indulgence? . . . .

'Nor is one class of society more base than another in this respect. The highest social life is often the most vile in its secret history. A young man at the age of twenty-one takes possession of his portion of the paternal estate, erects a house upon it, where he retires and establishes a household for himself. He secures what means of gratification his taste can select, and thus lives, sometimes ten or fifteen years, if no heiress or beauty cross his path of sufficient attractions to induce him to add her as an ornamental appendage to his establishment. Meanwhile his human "property" steadily increases, both in numbers and value; for the lighter the mulatto, the more desirable among the fastidious: and rare beauty is often the result of a *second* intermingling of the same aristocratic blood with the offspring of a former passion. From time to time, friends come to visit this bachelor hall, and in due season the master is repaid for his hospitality to them by a valuable addition to his stock of human chattels. . . . .

'Peace and happiness, and the faith which is as immovable as the everlasting hills in the heart of pure and constant love, those essential elements of the true home, are nowhere to be found in slavery. The wife constantly sees the likeness of her husband in children that are not hers; the husband welcomes every new-comer among them as so many hundreds of prospective gain, and devotes himself to their increase, while his legal children are born with feeble minds and bodies, with just force enough to transmit the family name, and produce in feebler characters a second edition of the father's life. The plantation in Virginia is "stocked" with negroes that are bought with sole reference to their capacities for reproduction, and master and slave unite, the former consciously, the latter unconsciously, in the same odious enterprise of raising victims for the southern market.'—*Tract: Influence of Slavery upon the White Population.*

KIDNAPPING.

The dangers to which free persons of colour are exposed by entering a slave state doubtless tends to fix the coloured population in a particular spot, and to render them suspicious of overtures of employment from strangers; for they may be unwittingly transported to one of the nearest slave states, and there sold. The following are cases in illustration:

The first case is that of Solomon Northrup, a negro who was kidnapped in a very extraordinary manner. In the year 1841, Northrup lived at Saratoga Springs, in the state of New York; he was then thirty-four years of age, and had a wife and three children. He was a clever, handy person; could drive a carriage, play on the fiddle, and make himself generally useful. One day, two strangers, named Merrill and Russell, were introduced to him. They spoke of being connected with a travelling-circus, and required an assistant possessing Northrup's accomplishments. The wages offered were fair—a dollar a day, and expenses till he returned. Pleased with the offer, Solomon hired himself to the strangers; and bidding good-bye for a short time to his wife and family, mounted the box of a travelling-carriage, and drove off on his journey. The party went first to the city of New York, and there Northrup expressed a disinclination to proceed southward; but being finally persuaded to go, he took the precaution to procure from the custom-house papers certifying his being a freeman; and forthwith went off with his employers through New Jersey and Pennsylvania to Baltimore, in Maryland, and thence to Washington. Here, Northrup was told he would see the circus company, and be employed with his violin. The party, meanwhile, conducted him to a tavern, to get some refreshments—an arrangement to which, of course, he could have no objection. He ate and drank unreservedly. The drugged liquor did its work, and he soon became sick, and, finally, insensible. How long he remained in this condition, he could not tell; but when he came to his senses, he found himself handcuffed in a slave-pen, with his legs fettered to a ring in the floor. In reply to his alarmed and indignant questions, he was told that he was a runaway slave from Georgia. It was vain to assert that he was a freeman, from the state of New York; his remonstrances were met by threats of the lash. What could the unfortunate negro do? His coat, hat, money, and free papers had been taken from him. Continuing to remonstrate, he was actually whipped with a cat-o'-nine-tails, and otherwise beaten in a savage manner, with the view, possibly, of breaking his spirit, and rendering him submissive. He was now left to ruminate over his hapless condition; and after a confinement of a few days, carried off with a number of other negroes, by steam-boat and railway, to Norfolk, in Virginia; from which place he was shipped with his companions to New Orleans. Here he was sold to a planter, to go up to Red River; and was subsequently purchased twice, and kept in slavery for a period of nearly twelve years, up to January 3, 1853. He was on that day unexpectedly set at liberty, and returned to his family.

After Merrill and Russell had fraudulently disposed of Northrup, and pocketed the sum for which they had sold him, they returned northward, and carried on similar practices with other negroes whom they inveigled into their power. Their tricks were at length discovered; and it was probably through this circumstance that Northrup regained his liberty. The two kidnappers were taken into custody, and brought for examination before the justices at Ballston Spa, on the 11th of July 1854. Northrup, and other witnesses, appeared against them; and it is from the narrative of this judicial inquiry, in a Saratoga newspaper, that we have gathered the foregoing facts. The parties accused did not deny the charge; but claimed their release on account of the Statute of Limitations, requiring an indictment to be found within three years of the commission of the offence. The district-attorney, in reply, maintained that the offence was committed up till the day that Northrup was set at liberty, in January 1853. The magistrates, taking the same view of the case, remanded Merrill and Russell to prison, to await the course of law. And the last thing we hear of them is, that they were held to bail by Northrup in the sum of 5000 dollars, to answer in a civil suit of personal damages for having sold him into slavery.

A number of the *New York Evening Post* (Mr Bryant's ably conducted paper), copies the following case of kidnapping from the *Cincinnati Columbian* of January 4, 1855. We give it exactly as it is therein related:

'A deeply interesting reunion of a severed family took place at the house of Mr Levi Coffin on last Saturday. The story, as told us by the parties, runs in this wise: Forty-eight years ago, two little coloured boys, named Peter and Levin Still, were playing in the highway near their father's house, on the Delaware river, when a stranger passing by in a gig, asked them to take a ride. The boys did so; and were thus kidnapped, and carried to Lexington, Kentucky, where they were sold to one John Fisher. They were ultimately sold to other masters; and after thirteen years' slavery in Kentucky, were sent south, where they were purchased by John Hogan, of Franklin county, South Alabama. At the age of twenty-four, Levin died; but Peter continued a slave for thirty-one years. During this period, he married a female slave belonging to one Barnard M'Kinon, a neighbour of his master, and had three children—two sons and a daughter. By years of extreme economy, Peter at last saved 500 dollars. This was enough to purchase his freedom; and a worthy Jewish gentleman, acting for Peter, paid the money.

'Peter bade farewell to his family, and went north, to Philadelphia, to discover his relatives. He found his aged mother and eight brothers and sisters still living. He laboured for some time to save enough to buy the freedom of his wife and family; but as his accumulations were slow, and the amount to be raised very large— 5000 dollars—he at last determined to appeal to the charitable public for aid. He went from place to place, telling his story, and asking assistance. In the meantime, his family ran away from their master; travelling at night, and remaining concealed in the daytime, they escaped from the slave states to Indiana, where, however, they were captured by a white man, who returned them to their master.

'On being taken back, they became hopeless of ever getting free. At last, after four years of effort, Peter had raised the 5000 dollars; and a few weeks ago, an agent was despatched to Alabama. He purchased the wife and children, and brought them on to this city, to which Peter had come from Philadelphia to meet them. The reunion was deeply affecting. One of the sons is twenty-seven, and the other twenty-four years of age. One of them had a wife in Alabama, who died, leaving a baby only a few months old. When coming away, the father begged hard for this little one, but it was worth 200 dollars: he had nothing, and came away without it. If these are fair samples, southern slaves have not been so much degraded and brutalised as is sometimes represented. Peter expects, when he reaches Philadelphia, to publish a card of thanks to those who have aided him. He and his family will leave this morning.'

AN OPULENT SLAVEHOLDER.

In the summer of 1854 there appeared a communication in a Richmond newspaper, giving an account of a Mr Samuel Hairston, a planter, who is described as the wealthiest man in Virginia, if not in the United States. The account, which we copy, will be read with interest. 'I have thought for some time I would write for your paper something in relation to the richest man in Virginia, and the largest slaveholder in the Union, and perhaps in the world, unless the serfs of Russia be considered slaves; and the wish expressed in your paper, a few days ago, to know who was so wealthy in Virginia, induces me to write this now. Samuel Hairston, of Pittsylvania, is the gentleman. When I was in his section a year or two ago, he was the owner of between 1600 and 1700 slaves, in his own right, having but a little while before taken a census. He also has a prospective right to about 1003 slaves more, which are now owned by his mother-in-law, Mrs R. Hairston, he having married her only child. He now has the management of them, which makes the number of his slaves reach near 3000. They increase at the rate of nearly 100 every year: he has to purchase a large plantation every year to settle them on. A large number of his plantations are in Henry and Patrick counties, Virginia. He has large estates in North Carolina. His landed property in Stokes alone is assessed at 600,000 dollars. His wealth is differently estimated at 3,000,000 to 5,000,000 dollars; and I should think it nearer the latter. You think he has a hard lot; but, I assure you, Mr Hairston manages all his matters as easy as most would an estate of 10,000 dollars. He has overseers who are compelled to give him a written statement of what has been made and spent on each plantation, and his negroes are all clothed and fed from his own domestic manufacture; and raising his own tobacco-crop, which is immensely large, as so much clear gain every year besides his increase in negroes, which is a fortune of itself. And now for his residence. I have travelled over fifteen states of this Union, and have never seen anything comparable to his yard and garden, except some of those in the Mississippi delta, and none of them equal to it. Mrs Hairston has been beautifying it for years: and a good old minister, in preaching near the place, and describing paradise, said "it was as beautiful as Mrs Hairston's;" or, as a friend who visited Washington city for the first time, remarked that "the public grounds were nearly as handsome as Samuel Hairston's." He is a plain, unassuming gentleman, and has never made any noise in the world, though he could vie with the Brucos, the M'Donoughs, and Astors; and it is strange, that while their wealth is co-extensive with the Union, he is not known 100 miles from home. I believe he is now the wealthiest man in the Union, as William B. Astor is only worth about 4,000,000 dollars, and the estates of city people are vastly overrated, while Mr Hairston can show the property that will bring the cash at any moment. Mr Hairston was raised within a few miles of where he now lives, in Henry county. He has several brothers, who are pretty well to do in the world. One of them, Marshall Hairston, of Henry, owns more than 700 negroes; Robert Hairston, who now lives in Mississippi, near 1000; and Harden Hairston, who has also moved to Mississippi, about 600 slaves. George Hairston, of Henry, has given almost all of his property to his children, reserving only about 150 slaves for his own use. This, I believe, is a correct statement of the circumstances of the Hairston family.'

A COACH PASSENGER.

The following appears in the *Independent*, an American newspaper:

'While travelling not long ago in one of the south-western counties of Virginia, the following thrilling incident took place. Starting in the stage-coach soon after breakfast, the morning being a delightful one in the latter part of the month of May, I took my seat on the box by the side of the driver; and behind me, on the top, was seated a bright, intelligent-looking mulatto boy, apparently of eighteen or nineteen years of age. After being on the road a few minutes, I turned about and asked him where he was going. He replied, he was going down a few miles to live with Master ——, who kept the stage-house at the west stand; that he had lived with him the last summer, and that his master had sent him down to live with him the coming season. Turning from the boy, the driver remarked to me, in an under-tone: "The boy is deceived; I am taking him down to the slave-pen, a few miles on, where slaves are kept preparatory to being sent to Louisiana: this deception is practised to get him from his home and mother without creating a disturbance on the place." Shortly after, as we drew near to the place where the boy supposed he was to stop, he began to gather up, preparatory to leaving the stage, the few articles he had brought away from his home. The driver said to him, in a decided tone of voice: "You are not to get off the stage here."

'The boy, in astonishment, replied: "Yes, I is; I'se got a letter for Master ——. I'se going to live there this summer."

'By this time we had reached the house, and Master —— making his appearance, John—for that was the name of the boy—delivered his letter, and appealed to Master —— to be relieved from the command of the driver. The master made no reply, as this kind of deception was no new thing to him. After reading the letter and folding it up, he was about putting it into his pocket, when it flashed on the mind of the boy that he was sold, and was bound for the slave-pen.

'He exclaimed in agony: "Tell me, master, if I'se sold?"

'No reply was made.

'He exclaimed again: "Tell me, master, if I'se sold?"

'This last appeal brought the response: "Yes, John, you are sold."

'The boy threw himself back on the top of the stage, and, rolling in agony, sent up such a wail of wo as no one in the stage could endure: even the hotel-keeper walked away in shame, and the driver hurried into his box, and drove off in haste to drown the noise of his cry. The passengers were all deeply moved at the distress of the boy, and tried in various ways to soothe his wounded and crushed spirit, but his agony was beyond the reach of their sympathy. When his agony had somewhat abated, he exclaimed: "Oh, if they had only let me bid my mother good-bye! They have lied to me! They have lied to me! If they had a' told me I was sold, and I could a' bid my mother good-bye, I'd a' gone without making them trouble, hard as it is!" By this time we had passed on some two or three miles since leaving the last stand, when, drawing near to a pretty thick wood, the boy became tranquil. Waiting till we had entered the wood a few rods, he darted from the top of the stage, and ran into the woods as agile as a deer, no doubt with the feeling that it was for his life. The driver instantly dropped his reins, and pursued the boy. Proving himself no match, he returned, exclaiming: "You see I have done what I could to catch him." He mounted his box and drove on a mile or so, when he reined up his horses to a house, and, calling to the keeper, asked: "Where are your sons?"

'He replied, they left home that morning with the dogs, to hunt a negro, and would not be home before night. The driver said to him, that Mr —— had sent his boy John on the stage that morning, to be delivered at the pen, and that he had jumped from the top of the stage and taken to the woods. His reply was: "We will hunt him for you to-morrow." The driver said he wished only to notify him of his being in the woods.

'As we drove on, I made inquiry: "How long have you driven a stage on this road?"

'He replied: "About fifteen years."

"Do you frequently take down negroes to this slave-pen?"

"Yes, frequently."

"What will become of this boy John?"

'He replied: "He will skulk about the woods until he is nearly starved, and will some night make his way up to his master's house, and in about two weeks I shall bring him down again to the slave-pen in handcuffs." After a pause, even this driver, feeling his degradation in being the instrument of such misery, broke out in the exclamation: "This is a cursed business; but in this case this is not the worst feature in it: the man who sold him is his own father!"'

APPENDIX.

FUGITIVE SLAVE LAW.

Since the passing of this law, a considerable number of seizures under its provisions have taken place in the northern states; though in Massachusetts and some other states, from resolutions adopted on the subject, it will in future be scarcely possible to apply the law without producing a collision between federal and state authorities.

One of the most noted cases of seizure was that of Anthony Burns, who was carried off from Boston in May 1854; a large military force being required to aid the federal officers on the occasion. Burns was afterwards purchased from his owner, and restored to liberty. Philadelphia has obtained an unfortunate distinction for the manner in which the law has been strained to secure fugitives. The harsh treatment of a gentleman in that city, Mr Passmore Williamson, who was imprisoned for some months on a frivolous charge connected with the case of an alleged fugitive woman and her family, will be in every one's recollection.

The latest fugitive slave case coming under our notice is that of Thomas, a mulatto, seized at Philadelphia in January 1857. A letter from that city, in the *Anti-slavery Standard,* gives the following narrative:

'Our city has been disgraced by another fugitive slave case. I had half hoped that we were to witness no more of these revolting spectacles; but this was, of course, looking for too much. As long as we have fugitive slaves and a fugitive slave law—fugitive slave-officers and fugitive slave-courts—and on our borders, slave-breeders, slave-traders, and professional slave-catchers, we shall not be without liability to a recurrence of those outrages. The particulars of this last case you will find in the newspaper reports of the proceedings, several of which I herewith send you. The chief facts are these:

'On Thursday last, a young mulatto man, of about twenty years of age, was arrested in this city as the property of a William H. Gatchell of Baltimore. The parties who apprehended him were Deputy Marshals Jenkins and Crossin—the same that were so disgracefully connected with the outrage perpetrated on the fugitive Thomas, several years ago, at Wilkesbarre. They seized him on a warrant issued by David Paul Brown, jun., who, it appears, has been appointed, since the death of the infamous Ingraham, a United States commissioner. This David Paul Brown, jun., is a son of the lawyer of the same name, who, in times past, won for himself an honourable reputation as a champion of freedom, but whose character, in this respect, it must be confessed, has of late days lost a good deal of its lustre. There are associations, however, still connected with the name which could not fail to give rise to astonishment, when the facts were announced that an alleged slave had been arrested under a warrant from David Paul Brown, jun., and that David Paul Brown, jun., was the commissioner who was to sit in judgment upon the case. "Who is this David Paul Brown, jun.?" was a question that was in every one's mouth. "Is it true that he is a son of our old friend, David Paul Brown, the man who used to scathe with such eloquent indignation all aiders and abettors in this infamous business?" Of course, there was but one answer to be given to these interrogatories. You can well imagine the expressions of surprise and disgust with which that answer would be received.

'The counsel for the slave-catcher was also a new man in this dirty business. From some of his antecedents, perhaps, there was nothing better to be expected; but from his looks, almost any one would have supposed that he would have recoiled from an offer to engage his services for so base a purpose. His name is Daniel Dougherty; he is an Irishman by birth, and a pseudo-democrat in politics. These two circumstances would naturally suggest the probability of his sympathies being on the side of the slaveholder; but from his ingenuous countenance and upright and manly port, one could hardly fail to infer a heart that would spurn a fee from the hand of a low-lived slave-catcher. But Mr Dougherty did not seem to be troubled with any of the qualms of weak humanity. He conducted his case with the utmost *sang froid*, and laboured to send an innocent man to endless slavery, with less apparent emotion than many a humane person would exhibit in inflicting a slight punishment on a convicted criminal.

'The counsel for the prisoner was William S. Peirce, Esq., an able lawyer and a conscientious man. For many years, Mr Peirce has been the most prompt and efficient lawyer we have had in Philadelphia in cases of this kind. He is always ready to act when called upon, and never fails to exert himself to the utmost for his client and for the cause involved. In this case, he even excelled himself, leaving no expedient untried which held out any hope of foiling the oppressor and rescuing the victim. He appealed to the humanity of the commissioner and to his respect for legal precedent; he shewed a palpable informality in the preliminary proceedings, and urged the justifiableness and the duty of giving to the prisoner the benefit of the irregularities; but his appeals and his proof of defective forms were alike unavailing. Mr Brown decided the case by declaring the man to be the property of his claimant, and issuing a warrant for his rendition.

'For his services in this act of mock-judicial outrage, Commissioner Brown will receive the price of blood—ten dollars—together with the thanks, doubtless, of the Judas who employed him. He will, also, on the other hand, have the execrations of the unhappy victim of his decision, and the contempt or pity of all good men who are or may be cognizant of the transaction. He may try to persuade himself that he has only been discharging a conscientious duty; but he will not succeed. He knows that he voluntarily assumed the duties of his office; and he knew, when he solicited and accepted his appointment, that one of its functions would be to sit in judgment on innocent men, wickedly put on trial for their liberty. If *he* may lay the flattering unction to his soul that he is but executing the law, and therefore without blame, so may Graham, the Baltimore slave-catcher, to whom he granted his warrant; so may Alberti; so may every professional slave-catcher and duly appointed hangman that snaps the "nippers" on his victim's wrists, or slips a noose on the platform of a gallows.

'This base outrage was perpetrated in a manner and by instruments altogether becoming its character. Official insolence, and a disregard of decent usage, characterised its performance from beginning to end. It was a sad spectacle; and that too, not so much from the mute despair of the wretched victim thus robbed of all that was dear to him, as from the mute indifference of the 400,000 people who make up the population of this great city. It is melancholy and depressing to observe how little sensation an atrocious incident of this kind excites in this great and loud-professing metropolis. We have churches and Quaker meeting-houses, and thousands upon thousands of religious professors of every variety of creed, but how few of them all feel any concern for the wrongs of the slave, or the cruel injustice of the oppressor. It is true that yesterday the Rev. Dr Furness made this case the subject of a touching sermon to his people, and Lucretia Mott preached upon it faithfully at the meeting which she attends; and doubtless there were some others occupying similar positions who were not unmindful of their duty in this regard; but the great mass of our ministers and their hearers, our editors and their readers, care for none of these things. The slave is manacled in our midst, and how few there are to lay it to heart!'

UNDERGROUND RAILROAD.

It need hardly be explained what is meant by this phrase. Over the extensive district of country from the borders of the slave states to Canada, there are places known to negroes where they will receive aid to help them on their way to the land of freedom. Unable to read, and exposed to great dangers, the fugitives generally avoid roads, and hold on their course according to certain landmarks by day, and the north star by night. Such is the Underground Railroad. Exciting narratives descriptive of escapes are constantly appearing in northern newspapers.

The following appears in the *Syracuse Standard*, a newspaper of the state of New York:

'The Underground Railroad occasionally brings out rich things. Yesterday a beautiful mulatto woman from the Maryland shore, near Baltimore, called upon Mr Loguen. She was a fugitive from high-life in slavedom. Her dress, address, and conversation, shewed she had been valued and cared for. She naturally inquired into the quality and amount of business at the Syracuse Depôt. Mrs Loguen took the record of the names of the fugitives that had called at her house, and commenced reading them.

'"That is the name of my husband," she exclaimed with enthusiasm, when a certain name was read.

'Mr and Mrs Loguen instantly called to mind an accomplished semi-coloured man they had sent on to Rev. Mr Mausfield & Co., at Auburn, three weeks ago. She told her story as follows:

'She had been married about six weeks. Her husband and herself were house-slaves of two notable and wealthy families in Maryland, and were greatly attached. About three weeks since, her master suspected that she intended to escape with her husband, and arrested her, and put her in jail. She managed to notify her husband of her case, and he instantly fled to avoid a similar fate, and probable sale to the far South. Her mistress and daughter were greatly attached to her, and procured her release, and in three days thereafter she fled on foot to Philadelphia, with the aid of the man who helped her husband off. Anti-slavery men put her on the road, and now for the second time she has got track of her husband.

'Mr Loguen at once thought it his duty to go to Auburn with her, and help to find her husband. On arrival at Auburn, he placed her in the parlour of one of the best hotels, and called on Mr Mansfield, who went with him to another clergyman to whom he was directed. He was at meeting, and Mr Loguen saw a coloured man in a distant part of the meeting who resembled the fugitive, and sent a person to bring him to the lobby to see Mr Loguen. The poor man was seized with a tremor. The fact was, he was an excellent machinist, and instead of going to Canada, had hired out at good wages at Auburn rather, as instructed to do by Mr Loguen, if he found a chance.

"They are after you, Fred," said Mr Loguen; "but hold up your head—I'll take you where you won't be hurt."

"Who is after me?"

"Who but your master could be here after you? But don't be scared. Follow me, and you will be safe."

"Can you fight?"

"It depends on whom I am to fight."

"Will you fight slaveholders if they have come to take you?"

"Yes—I would fight a regiment of them."

'By this time they arrived at the hotel, and Mr Loguen proceeded directly to the parlour, which was richly furnished and gas-lighted. The fellow's feelings were worked up to the highest point by being led to such a place, where he could expect to see no one but a slaveholder. On entering the room, he saw his beautiful wife alone. He was so overcome that he almost fell to the floor, exclaiming at the same time: "It is my wife!" They rushed together, and a happier bride and bridegroom could not be found in the world—we'll venture to say.'

TAKE HIM, DEAD OR ALIVE.

The *New York Tribune*, of February 24, 1857, has the following:

'We find, in a North Carolina paper, the following advertisement, which presents a curious illustration of slaveholding law and slaveholding manners:

"STATE OF N. CAROLINA, JONES COUNTY.—Whereas complaint upon oath hath this day been made to us, Adonijah McDaniel and John N. Hyman, two of the Justices of the Peace of said county, by Franklin B. Harrison of said county, planter, that a certain male slave belonging to him, named Sam, hath absented himself from his master's services, and is lurking about said county, committing acts of felony and other misdeeds. These are, therefore, in the name of the State, to command the said slave forthwith to surrender himself and return home to his master, and we do hereby require the Sheriff of said County of Jones to make diligent search and pursuit after the said slave, and him having found, to apprehend and secure, so that he may be conveyed to his said master, or otherwise discharged as the law directs; and the said Sheriff is hereby authorised and empowered to raise and take with him such power of his county as he shall think fit for apprehending the said slave; and we do hereby, by virtue of the Act of Assembly in such case provided, intimate and declare that if the said slave, named Sam, doth not surrender himself and return home immediately after the publication of these presents, *that any person may kill and destroy the said slave, by such means as he or they may think fit, without accusation or impeachment of any crime or offence for so doing, and without incurring any penalty and forfeiture thereby.*

"Given under our hands and seals the 29th day of September, A.D. 1856.—A. McDANIEL, J. P.   J. N. HYMAN, J. P.

"$100 REWARD.

"I will give Fifty Dollars for the apprehension and delivery of the said boy to me, or lodge him in any Jail in the State so that I get him, or One Hundred Dollars for his head.

"*Oct.* 1*st*, '56.   F. B. HARRISON."

'Fifty dollars for the person of "the said boy" Sam, but one hundred dollars for his head, the killing of him, "without incurring any penalty or forfeiture thereby," being fully authorised in a legal document under the hands and seals of two justices of the peace! Even if Sam reads the newspapers, and the above proclamation should come to his knowledge, no reasonable man would advise him to give himself up under it. It is not so much the danger, if he did so, of being whipped to death by the amiable Mr F. B. Harrison, who is evidently in a considerable state of excitement, as the certainty that in a community that tolerates the publication of such advertisements, there must be plenty of sportsmen who would jump at the chance of shooting a negro, to say nothing of the hundred dollars to be got by doing so; and as there is no time limited within which he is to deliver himself up, this right of killing, without incurring any penalty or forfeiture, must be considered as accruing from the very issue of the proclamation. However, there is no restriction on the way of doing the deed, the volunteer executioner, under this act, being allowed the choice of "any means" that may be thought fit.'

NEGRO DOGS.

The following is an exact copy of an advertisement from a negro-dog tracker, in the *Lexington Democratic Advocate;* Lexington being in Missouri, near the borders of Kansas. The advertisement appeared during the Kansas troubles, in 1855:

'NEGRO DOGS.—I would inform the citizens of Holmes County that I still have my NEGRO DOGS, and that they are in good training, and ready to attend to all calls of hunting and catching RUN-AWAY NEGROES, at the following rates. For hunting per day, five dollars, or if I have to travel any distance, every day will be charged for, in going and returning, as for hunting, and at the same rates. Not less than five dollars will be charged in any case, where the Negroes come in before I reach the place. From fifteen to twenty-five dollars will be charged for catching, according to the trouble; if the Negro has weapons, the charge will be made according to the difficulty had in taking him, or in case he kills some of the dogs, the charge will not be governed by the above rates. I am explicit to prevent any misunderstanding. The owner of the slave to pay all expenses in all cases. I venture to suggest to any person having a slave

runaway, that the better plan is to send for the dogs forthwith when the negro goes off, if they intend sending at all, and let no other person go in the direction, if they know which way the runaway went; as many persons having other negroes to hunt over the track, and failing of success, send for the dogs, and then perhaps fail in consequence to catch their negro, and thus causelessly fault the dogs. Terms cash. If the money is not paid at the time the negro hunted for is caught, he will be held bound for the money. I can be found at home at all times, five and a half miles east of Lexington, except when hunting with the dogs. JOHN LONG.
Feb. 14, 1855.'

SLAVE HEROISM.

The following was communicated by a correspondent to the *New York Tribune:*

'In November last [1855], while on a tour in the southern states, on account of my business connections in Vermont and Massachusetts, upon the plantation of Mr G. W——, in Wayne County, Mississippi, a negro, for some trifling offence, as pretending sickness, was sentenced to twenty-five lashes, on the bare back, to be given at his plantation, in presence of his wife, and all the other slaves. He was tied, hand and foot, in a most painful manner, in a dark hole, called the "black hole," until the punishment was inflicted, which was done in the most inhuman manner. After an attempt, and only for appearance' sake, to cure his wounds, he was dismissed to the field, in a miserable condition. In about a week, he was strong enough to avail himself of an opportunity offered him to escape; and, taking no clothing but what was absolutely necessary, he went to a large swamp in the vicinity; and, in about two hours, he heard the horrid braying of blood-hounds, or, as they call them, "negro dogs." After most terrible agony for forty-eight hours, and the slightest possible chance of escape, he was left alone; and then commenced his trials. In a state the most inhuman in the Union, with no friends to assist him, not even the necessaries of life, *I met him*. I gave him a suit of clothes, some money, and by dint of concealment in the daytime, and only travelling at night, he passed through Kentucky, and arrived in the land of freedom—that is, on the borders of *Ohio*—in January 1855. The weather was intensely cold, his feet horribly frosted, his clothes torn to shreds, but his heart uplifted by the hope of liberty. Meeting some kind friends, as they always do in Cincinnati, he was working manfully in a secret place, to obtain money to go to Canada; and by this time he is well on the way, or I would fear to expose his whereabouts. I have since heard from a friend of mine there, that his wife received ten lashes for aiding in his escape. He is determined to coin enough money to buy his faithful wife, and both to live in a free state, where slaveholders and blood-hounds are not the boast of the community.'

SLAVE-WHIPPING IN MISSOURI.

A gentleman travelling through the states west of the Mississippi, sent lately to a New York newspaper the following account of an incident which came under his notice, in Lexington, Missouri:

'In the morning of the 21st February 1856,' he says, 'I was, for the first time in my life, a spectator of the sale of slaves. Two young men and a girl, about eighteen years of age, were placed upon the block, surrounded by forty or fifty slaveholders. The first put up was a "nigger" of great beauty and fine form. The auctioneer commenced by exhorting the farmers to remember that the hemp was all down—hands were scarce—niggers had taken a rise; and told them that there stood one of the best-looking niggers in the state; that he was a slave for life, and had no wife to trouble him —was sound—had good teeth and eyes; in short, was an "excellent nigger!" The bidding proceeded until 1250 dollars was reached, and the hammer fell upon the nigger, who was led away by the highest bidder. During the sale, the auctioneer and others indulged in witticisms and puns upon the boy, which set the crowd to laughing; but the slave did not laugh. Not a smile nor a tear did I notice during the whole time. His expression was that of deep despondency.

'Being called away, I did not see the other two sold. Several others were sold in that place during the same week at Sheriff's sale. On the succeeding Friday, a scene was presented in that same court-house which almost beggars description.

'Sheriff Withers, having a "nigger woman," who, on the previous day, had been neglectful of her taskwork, sent for a blacksmith to come and chastise her. He came, bolted the door, tied the woman's hands together, and lashed them over her head to the ceiling, and commenced whipping. The screams of the woman brought her husband to the rescue. He broke open the door, and with a butcher-knife in his hand, rushed forward to cut his wife loose. The slave and blacksmith encountered each other, and in the affray the latter got his arm cut. The slave finally surrendered, and was led away to the jail, while the woman received a double whipping. These are the facts in the case.

'News of this "horrible outrage" was soon circulated, and the excitement became intense. At four o'clock, the mob, numbering two or three hundred, moved towards the court-house. The "boy" —a quadroon of about forty years of age—was brought into the building and placed within the bar. Colonel Reed was called to preside, and Colonel Walton explained the object of the meeting.

'He said: "A great crime has been committed—an outrage upon one of our citizens by a nigger. We have come together, not to imbrue our hands in the blood of innocence; but rebellion of slaves is becoming common. Something must be done to put a stop to it, to protect our wives, our children, and our sacred homes."

'A member of the legislature earnestly remonstrated against mob-law, and recommended that a day be appointed to whip the boy, and have all the slaves of the county present. He was not heard through, for the speech did not suit the mob. A committee of twelve was appointed to decide immediately what punishment the boy should receive. That committee retired, but soon returned, with Colonel Reed at their head, who read the following announcement:

'*Your committee have decided that the boy shall receive* ONE THOUSAND *lashes on his bare back, two hundred to be administered this evening (if he can bear it), and the remaining eight hundred from time to time, as in the judgment of the committee his physical nature can bear up under it. Also, we advise that a committee of three physicians be appointed to superintend the operation, and three citizens be chosen to whip him. Also, that the person whose arm was cut by the slave have the privilege of giving him the last two hundred lashes.*

'The report was almost unanimously adopted; the wretched slave was stripped of his clothing, and made to kneel down in front of Colonel Reed, while his hands, extending *over* the top of a bench, were tied to the floor.

'Let the reader now imagine Colonel Reed upon the bench, cigar in mouth, three honoured physicians on the right, and three burly slaveholders (whips in hand) on the left of a poor slave who was kneeling before them, with his whole person bared to the chilling atmosphere, the thermometer marking zero. Outside the bar are two or three hundred border-ruffians, all eager for blood. Such was the scene presented in the court-house of Lexington, in the state of Missouri, on the last Friday of February 1856.

'The whipping commenced. Colonel Reed sprang to his feet with curiosity; more than a hundred heads were peering in to get a sight of their miserable victim. But before a dozen lashes had been administered, the slave fell to the floor, bleeding and writhing in agony. The slaveholder struck the harder, and ordered him to get up. The physicians interfered, and felt his pulse, and declared that he could never stand such lashes.

'Some one cried out: "988 yet to come," and the whipping was resumed. Lash upon lash was inflicted, until *one hundred* had been given, when his whole back, from the top of his shoulders down to his very feet, was a mass of blood and mangled flesh.

'The whipping was continued without cessation, amid the most piteous and beseeching wails and cries, such as: "O gen'lemen, O gen'lemen, have mercy!" "O gen'lemen!" "O Lord!" "O Lord!" until they became fainter, and died away upon the ear.

'When they commenced giving him the second hundred, I left the room in anguish of spirit, exclaiming to myself: "Oh, that I were a dog, that I might not call man my brother!"

'He was not permitted to rise until the two hundred were given. He was taken out the next day, but it was decided he was too sore to whip. On the third day, he was taken out and whipped again in the presence of a large crowd; but when they had given him twenty, his strength completely failed him.

'Whether the whole of the thousand lashes were administered, or whether he gave out before receiving the complete penalty, I have no means of knowing; but I do know that some of the leading slaveholders pledged themselves to each other to carry it through, despite the indignation of a portion of the community and of the entreaties of his master, although at first the master had given him up to the mob heartily, and was even willing they should hang him.'

BRUTAL MURDER OF A SLAVE BY HIS OWNER.

'Michael Boylan, a German, residing on Lover's Lane, near this city, was arrested yesterday by Sergeant Wilson and Privates Richardson and Waller, of the mounted police, on a charge of whipping his own slave, a man named Stepney, to death. The circumstances of this outrage, as we have learned them, are as follows: It appears that the negro had been runaway for some time, and was taken on Tuesday last and carried to jail by Constable Jones. He was then whipped, and turned over to his master. Yesterday, Boylan, while under the influence of liquor, renewed the punishment, and continued it until the negro sank under the infliction, and died. When Sergeant Wilson arrived at the spot, the negro was lying on the ground lifeless, and Boylan by the side of him, completely stupified by liquor. The latter, together with his nephew, whose name we did not learn, were arrested and carried before Justice Russel, who committed them both to jail for further examination. Sergeant Wilson is of opinion that but for his prompt arrival on the spot, the negro would have been buried and the crime concealed, as the coffin was already prepared and a hole dug to receive it. We are shocked to record such a crime in our midst, and trust that the law will be rigidly enforced against the offender.'—*Savannah newspaper.*

THE INSURRECTIONS IN TENNESSEE.

From *The Memphis Appeal.*

At a meeting of the citizens of Sumner County, held at the Courthouse on Saturday, the 6th of December, 1856, Thomas C. Douglas, Wiley G. Douglas, and L. A. Edwards, were appointed chairmen, and Thomas T. T. Tabb, secretary.

The object of the meeting having been explained in very pertinent and appropriate remarks by Messrs John W. Head and Houston Solomon, it was resolved that the chairmen appoint a committee of twelve to consider the developments of an insurrection elicited from some of the leaders thereof, and to draft resolutions by Monday, 12 o'clock, when this meeting will meet again to receive or reject them, and to adopt some plan for the better security of the community; whereupon the chairmen appointed the following gentlemen the committee—namely, Albert Franklin, William Parker, Dr James E. Blackmore, Dr Raymond Head, J. Seawell Carr, Joseph Walton, Robert Myers, John W. Head, M. S. Singleton, W. L. Baber, Dr J. M. Porter, and Leonidas Baker.

The meeting then adjourned to Monday, 12 o'clock.

Monday, Dec. 8.—The meeting having been called to order, the committee reported the following resolutions, which were unanimously adopted:

1. *Resolved*, That we have the clearest evidence that there was a contemplated insurrection among a portion of the slaves of our county; in this we all concur, and that the present investigation by which the plot has in part been unravelled and known to exist, be carefully prosecuted until the whole plan is fully developed, and that such an investigation be set on foot in the various civil districts of the county by the magistrates thereof.

2. *Resolved*, That the various magistrates of the county hand over the leaders of the conspiracy to a jury of twelve slaveholders of this county, appointed by this meeting; which jury shall try said slaves, and deal with them as the interest of the community may require; said jury to adopt such regulations in regard to the trial as they think proper.

8. *Resolved,* That each civil district in the county meet and organise a sufficient patrol, or body of men, prepared for any emergency, whose duty it shall be to see that the negroes remain on their masters' premises at night and on the Sabbath, unless absent by written permission of the owner or hirer, designating the time they are to be absent, and the place they are to go to; that said patrol also perform such other services as the safety and peace of the community may require, and this organisation be kept up for thirty days.

4. *Resolved,* That in addition to the above regulations, each master patrol his own premises, see that his own slaves remain home at night and on the Sabbath; and that other negroes do not congregate with his.

5. *Resolved,* That no voluntary assemblage of negroes be permitted at night, or on the Sabbath, for any purpose, for twelve months to come.

6. *Resolved,* That during the Christmas holidays no slave be permitted to leave his master's premises, unless on business of the master or owner, and with his written permission, specifying the time, place, and business.

7. *Resolved,* That all citizens be vigilant in seeing that the laws relative to slaves, hiring their time, carrying arms, buying ardent spirits, assembling together, going off their masters' premises with white men and free persons of colour, talking to them in a manner calculated to excite discontent, trading with them, &c., be promptly executed.

8. *Resolved,* That we recommend that the law be rigorously enforced against free negroes, when found guilty of a violation of it; and that a vigilant watch be kept over their movements. Should any one or more of them in any community be a nuisance, then the community might take such steps in reference to them as it is regarded necessary for its peace and safety. No free persons of colour shall remove to and settle in this county.

9. *Resolved,* That there are persons in our midst who are selling liquor to slaves, in violation of the law, and we recommend all such to cease their traffic, and if not, they will be required to leave the county, or the severest penalties will be inflicted upon them.

On motion—*Resolved,* in addition, That no school be kept open for the education of negroes, whether free or slave.

Resolved, That if any of the jury (of twelve appointed now), under the second resolution, should fail to act, that the president of the meeting supply their places by others, and that we endorse all such appointments made by him.

Resolved, That the proceedings of the meeting be published in *The Sumner Flag, Union and American, Nashville Banner,* and *The Gazette,* and that a copy thereof be furnished to each magistrate in the county.

Having appointed the jury of twelve, in conformity with the second resolution, the meeting adjourned. (Signed) THOMAS C. DOUGLAS, WILEY G. DOUGLAS, L. A. EDWARDS.

APPENDIX.

PRICE OF SLAVES.

The price of slaves, as has been said, has risen considerably during the past two or three years, and is still rising. In a letter from Lexington, Georgia, December 2, 1856, to the *Augusta Chronicle*, the writer says:

'About 100,000 dollars' worth of property was sold here to-day—land and negroes. Some of the sales were ahead of anything we have ever heard. A negro girl, fifteen years old, sold for 1280 dollars; another girl, fourteen years old, sold for 1280 dollars; another girl, fourteen years old, for 1305 dollars; another girl, eighteen years old (in family way), for 1500 dollars; a boy, eighteen years old, for 1290 dollars; a fellow, twenty-two years old, for 1500 dollars. These negroes belonged to the estate of John Wynn, deceased, and were sold on a credit of twelve months. There were fifty-seven of Wynn's negroes sold to-day, and brought 44,026 dollars. Of these, a great number (more than ordinary) were women and children; and a few diseased and old sold low. It is also proper to state, that but few of these negroes were bought by the legatees, and *not one* of those of which we have mentioned specific prices. They were common negroes—field-hands.

'But the most extraordinary sales were of three negroes belonging to the estate of Mrs Mary Watson: Leah, a negro girl, sixteen years old, sold for 1525 dollars; Harriet, about twenty years old, and child in her arms, sold for 1840 dollars—term, twelve months. These prices appear incredible, but all who are disposed to doubt can be satisfied by referring to the Record of the Court of Ordinary of Oglethorpe County.'

In an article recommending the South to unite in defending its institutions, the *Charleston Mercury* offers the following explanations respecting the rise in the price of negroes:

'Cheapness of labour is essential to the material progress of every people; but this can only obtain with the abundance of supply. Now, slave-labour is, and ought to be, the cheapest kind of labour. It will only become otherwise, when foreign and hostile influences are made to bear against it. The abolition of the slave-trade, by cutting off the supply, tends to this result. Slaves were never before so high in the South. They have, within the last few years, advanced 50 per cent. in price, and, in some instances, even more. To what is this attributable? Is it to an increase in the value of their productions? We think not. Taking the three great staples—cotton, rice, and sugar—as the standards, we can discover no such increase in the profits of their culture as would warrant this advance. Indeed, it may well be doubted, whether planting, throughout the South, during the last ten years, has been as profitable as for the same preceding period. It has certainly not been more so; and the purchaser now of slaves, at six hundred dollars each, has no promise of better returns for their labour, than when he bought them at four hundred dollars. The slave can neither cultivate nor produce more now than formerly. Thus, so far as the planting interest is concerned, the anomaly is presented, of an advance in the market-value of the capital employed, without any corresponding increase in its profits. We must therefore seek elsewhere for the real cause of the present high price of slaves.

'The influx of gold from California, in swelling the cost of almost every species of property, necessarily affected that of slaves. But there is a reason deeper and beyond this: it is the *scarcity of,* as compared with the multiplying *demands for, labour;* demands, too, so imperative that they must be supplied at almost any cost. In the last few years, internal improvements in the South have been prosecuted on a scale greater than ever before. With the consciousness of her resources, has come the determination to develop them.'

THE NEGROES OF WASHINGTON.

'The coloured population voluntarily sustain several churches, schools, and mutual assistance and improvement societies, and there are evidently persons among them of no inconsiderable cultivation of mind. Among the police reports of the city newspapers, there was lately (April 1855) an account of the apprehension of twenty-four "genteel coloured men"—so they were described—who had been found by a watchman assembling privately in the evening, and been lodged in the watch-house. The object of their meeting appears to have been purely benevolent, and, when they were examined before a magistrate in the morning, no evidence was offered, nor does there seem to have been any suspicion that they had any criminal purpose. On searching their persons, there were found a Bible, a volume of *Seneca's Morals; Life in Earnest;* the printed constitution of a society, the object of which was said to be "*to relieve the sick, and bury the dead;*" and a subscription paper, *to purchase the freedom of Eliza Howard,* a young woman, whom her owner was willing to sell at 650 dollars. I can think of nothing that would speak higher for the character of a body of poor men, servants and labourers, than to find, by chance, in their pockets, just such things as these. And I cannot value that man as a countryman, who does not feel intense humiliation and indignation, when he learns that such men may not be allowed to meet privately together, with such laudable motives, in the capital city of the United States, without being subject to disgraceful punishment. Washington is, at this time, governed by the Know Nothings; and the magistrate, in disposing of the case, was probably actuated by a well-founded dread of secret conspiracies, inquisitions, and persecutions. One of the prisoners, a slave named Joseph Jones, he ordered to be flogged; four others, called in the papers free men, and named John E. Bennett, Chester Taylor, George Lee, and Aquila Barton, were sent to the workhouse; and the remainder, on paying costs of court and fines, amounting in the aggregate to one hundred and eleven dollars, were permitted to range loose again.'—*Olmsted's Journey in the Seaboard Slave States.*

AN INCIDENT IN KANSAS.

Among the many anecdotes now in circulation connected with affairs in Kansas, is the following, which we condense from the *Herald of Freedom,* a Kansas newspaper, January 10, 1857.

For some time, a number of free negroes have been residing among the Cherokee Indians, following various occupations, and intermarrying with the Indian women. A young man, son of a negro by one of these Indian wives, wandered lately into Kansas, where he procured employment as a groom at the stage-station on Strauger Creek. One day, while he was engaged at the door of the stable, two white men rode up to the place, and eyeing the young man, thought they might make a good booty—probably 1200 dollars —by carrying him off, and selling him. With this design, they entered into conversation with him; they charged him with being a fugitive slave from Platte County, and ordered him immediately to come along with them. This charge the lad denied, and refused to go with them. Threats were now used; and when a pistol was presented to intimidate him, he ran hurriedly to the house to find a gun with which to defend himself. As he went towards the house, one of the ruffians fired his revolver, and shot the poor young man in the left side. Fortunately, the bullet, from the position in which the assailant was standing, glanced outwardly, or it might have proved fatal. He reached the house, and getting a gun from it, chased one of the fellows till he disappeared down a ravine; then, returning, he managed to intercept the other, who piteously begged for mercy, and finally gave up a five-inch Colt's revolver. Thus free from an infamous attempt on his liberty, he found it necessary to attend to his wounded side. He went to Lawrence, where his wound being attended to, he soon recovered.

NEGROES AND MULATTOES KEEPING SLAVES.

Mr Olmsted, in travelling through Texas, arrived one night at a house where he learns some curious particulars respecting free negroes and mulattoes.

'At the house where we stopped—in which, by the way, we ate our supper by the light of pine-knots blazing in the chimney, with an apology for the absence of candles—we heard some conversation upon a negro of the neighbourhood, who had been sold to a free negro, and who refused to live with him, saying he wouldn't be a servant to a nigger. All agreed that he was right, although the man was well known to be kind to his negroes, and would always sell any of them who wished it. The slave had been sold because he wouldn't mind. "If I had a negro that wouldn't mind," said the woman of the house, "I'd break his head, or I'd sell him. I wouldn't have one about me." Her own servant was standing behind her. "I do think it would be better if there wasn't any niggers in the world, they do behave so bad, some of 'em. They steal just like hogs."

'We inquired about the free negroes of whom they were speaking, and were told that there were a number in the county, all mulattoes, who had come from Louisiana. Some of them owned many negroes, and large stocks. There were some white people, good-for-nothing people, that married in with them, but they couldn't live in Texas after it; all went over into Louisiana. They knew of no law excluding free negroes from the state; if there were any such law, no one here cared for it.

'This county has been lately the scene of events, which prove that it must have contained a much larger number of free negroes and persons of mixed blood than we were informed on the spot, in spite of the very severe statute forbidding their introduction, which has been backed by additional legislative penalties in 1856. Banded together, they have been able to resist the power, not only of the legal authorities, but of a local "Vigilance Committee," which gave them a certain number of hours to leave the state, and a guerrilla of skirmishes and murders has been carried on for many months, upon the banks of the Sabine, with the revival of the old names of "Moderators and Regulators," of the early Texans.

'The feud appears to have commenced with the condemnation, by a justice of the peace, of a free mulatto, named Samuel Ashworth, to receive twenty-five lashes, on a charge of malicious killing of his neighbour's hogs, and of impertinent talking. The Ashworths were a rich mulatto family, settled in Texas in the earliest days of the republic, and exempted by special mention from the operation of the law forbidding residence to free negroes. They are now three and four generations removed from black blood, and have had a reputation for great hospitality, keeping open house for all who call. The member of the family who was condemned to the indignity of being publicly whipped, rose upon his guard while in the hands of the sheriff, and escaped. In a few days after, he returned with a mulatto companion, and shot the man on whose testimony he was condemned. Upon this the Vigilance Committee was organised, and the sheriff, who was suspected of connivance at the escape of Ashworth, and all the Ashworth family with their relatives and supporters, summoned to leave the county on pain of death. On the other hand, all free men of colour on the border, to the number of one hundred and fifty, or more, joined with a few whites and Spaniards, formed an organised band, and defied the committee; and then ensued a series of assassinations, burnings of houses and saw-mills, and open fights. The Moderators, or committee-men, became strong enough to range the county, and demand that every man, capable of bearing arms, should join them, or quit the county on pain of death. This increased the resistance and the bloody retaliation, and, at the last accounts, they were laying regular siege to the house of a family who had refused to join them. Thirty families had been compelled to leave the county, and murders were still occurring every week. Among those killed were two strangers, travelling through the county; also the deputy-sheriff, and the sheriff himself, who was found concealed under the floor of a lonely house, with a quantity of machinery for the issue of false money, and instantly shot; the proprietor of the house, defending himself, revolver in hand, fell pierced with many balls. The aid of the military power of the state had been invoked by the legal authorities; but the issue I have not seen in the newspapers.'

We take this opportunity of recommending for perusal the two excellent works of Mr Olmsted—*Journey in the Seaboard Slave States*, and *A Journey through Texas*. (London: Sampson Low; New York: Dix and Edwards.)

VOTING AT ELECTIONS.

On this subject, an article appears in *Putnam's Monthly* (a New York magazine), for November 1856. The writer, in lamenting that respectable persons should systematically refuse to take part in elections, makes the following observations:

'The whole white male population of the United States, for

instance, over twenty-one years of age, and, to be presumed, entitled to vote, is about 5,100,000; and yet the votes cast at a presidential election seldom exceed 3,100,000; leaving two millions of inhabitants who do not use their franchise. In the state of New York, in 1852, the voting population exceeded 800,000, yet the votes returned did not exceed 500,000. In Massachusetts, where there are more people, comparatively, capable of forming an opinion than in any other state in the Union, the white males, over twenty-one, are nearly 300,000; and yet the vote, in 1852, was only 133,000; shewing that nearly two-thirds of the adult population, for some cause or other, had stayed away from the polls. And the proportion is nearly as great in several other states. Some of these delinquents are, of course, kept away by illness, others by engagements abroad, but the majority, we have no doubt, by their own voluntary indifference and neglect.' The writer adds: 'The effect is, that the polls are controlled by interested or inferior persons, who get themselves or their fellows into important trusts, and shape the laws, and the administration of the laws, to suit their own debased purposes. They increase the taxes, they dispense jobs, they peculate in the public funds, they degrade the entire business and character of office, and arrange elections so as to secure a kind of hereditary tenure for themselves and their friends. But, suddenly, by some tremendous malfeasance, the community is aroused, and it looks with extreme surprise upon the enormity to which abuses have been carried. Why, however, should it be surprised? Was anything else to be expected? If the best men of society—well-informed and upright men—withdraw from a participation in public affairs, leaving them to any and all sorts of cliques, or to professional jobbers, who manage primary meetings and conventions, have they any one to blame but themselves? If the clergyman and the scholar, if the lawyer and the merchant, if the peaceable mechanic and the honest labourer, refuse to take an active part in nominating and choosing good representatives, they cannot complain that the rowdy and the ballot-stuffer take advantage of their remissness.'

It might have been added that the principal reason why respectable persons absent themselves from elections in some of the large cities, is the dread of suffering personal outrage; and on this account, they, surely, have good cause for complaint that the 'rowdies and ballot-stuffers' are not promptly dealt with by the authorities. In consequence of the outrages at the polls at the last elections in New York, the recorder of that city thus addressed the grand jury on the subject (Nov. 1856):

'Within the present week, our city has been the scene of outrages at the polls which are humiliating to us as citizens, and disgraceful to those having the power to check them. In the first ward of this city, and almost within hearing of the office of the mayor and chief of police, from the opening to the closing of the polls, there was one constant scene of riot and bloodshed. Respectable citizens, who went peaceably to the polls to deposit their votes, were knocked down and dragged through the streets without any interference on the part of the police to prevent the outrages. Hundreds were driven from the polls by an organised band of desperadoes, who openly refused to allow the electors to deposit a vote, unless it contained the name of a certain candidate.

'I have made these remarks that you may the better appreciate the necessity of prompt action on your part in certain cases which will be presented for your consideration. I will here add, that a large number of the police force was withdrawn from the first ward by order of the mayor of our city, and that a large number of the police force was on furlough on the day of election, and were engaged in advancing the interests of certain candidates, instead of being engaged in keeping the peace at the polls.'

VOTING IN SLAVE STATES.

Some strange disclosures occasionally take place respecting the system of voting at elections in the slave states. A person named Underwood was lately under the necessity of advertising his property for sale, and quitting Virginia, in consequence of displeasing the popular opinion. The case of T. Stannard, as told by himself in a letter to the *Newhaven Palladium*, Nov. 18, 1856, is worth narrating.

'I formerly resided at Fair Haven, where my family are now, and ever have been; but having myself been engaged for several years past in the commission business in Norfolk [Virginia], and having paid taxes there, and to the best of my abilities discharged my duties as a citizen of that place, I have considered it my residence—and in the spring of 1855, I offered to vote at their election, when, upon a full statement of my case to the proper authority, and with their knowledge that my family were here, it was decided that I was entitled to vote there, and I did so.

'I have never in any way meddled with the subject of slavery—having no inclination, nor, as I believed, any right to do so—consequently there has been no ill-feeling towards me on that account.

'Before the election, many political meetings were held in Norfolk, but I did not attend any of them, nor did I converse with any one on the subject, except on one occasion, in answer to an inquiry made by a friend, and then for a moment only. But although neither an abolitionist nor a politician, I examined the subject as a question of duty, for me as well as for every citizen of the United States, and I made up my mind that the election of Fremont would be best for all sections of the country, and determined to vote for him—not dreaming that, under our republican government, and in the democratic state of Virginia, any one would question my right to do so.

'On the day of election, I heard one gentleman ask another at the post-office who he should vote for, and he replied: "For John C. Fremont"—and the other said he should do so too. They may not have been in earnest, but I then supposed they were, and I had no reason to doubt that others would vote the same way; and in the afternoon I wrote a vote for Fremont and Dayton, and went to the place of voting. My right to vote was again examined, and on a statement of my case it was admitted, and I then, as the rules require, wrote my name on the back of my vote, and handed it to the inspector, who, as is customary, read aloud my first name, and then the names of my candidates. As soon as he declared that I voted for John C. Fremont, a large number of voices from the crowd shouted: "Hang him—hang him;" and the inspector handed me my vote, and said: "There is no such ticket voted here: we cannot receive this." I replied: "Very well," and took my vote again.

Some threats, which in the confusion that took place I did not distinctly understand, were made by those standing near me; and the presiding officer exclaimed: "Don't touch this man;" and then said to two persons who were, I presume, policemen: "Take him away from the polls."

'The officers seized hold of me, and hurried me through the crowd, and then left me; and I proceeded through a violent storm of wind and rain to my boarding-house, and from thence to my store. I afterwards returned to the house; and when at the supper-table, I heard persons speak of the vote which had been offered at the polls for Fremont, those who spoke of it not knowing by whom the vote was offered, and therefore speaking freely of it in my presence. From what I saw and heard at the polls, and what was said at the table, I was apprehensive that I had misunderstood my right as an American citizen, and that I had, though unconsciously, so offended public sentiment by my vote, as to be in danger of popular violence, and I therefore went from the table to my room, and locked the door.

'Soon after, I heard some one inquire for me; and the landlady sent a servant to my door to say that a gentleman wished to see me. On learning that he was alone, I invited him to my room; and he said that he came by request of another person—whom he named—to ask me if I had offered to vote for Fremont. I replied: "Yes." He then inquired: "What was your motive?" And I told him that I conscientiously believed it my duty to do so. He then said: "I am requested to advise you not to appear in the street to-night;" and I replied that I should not go out of the house. He retired, but soon after returned, and said: "Mr F—— wishes to see you at the door." I told him that I should not leave my room that night, but if Mr F—— wished to see me, he might come to my room. He then left me, and another person came to my door, and informed me that Mr F—— was not at the front door, but that several men, whom he named, were there; and I knew those men to be some of the most desperate characters in Norfolk.

'This was in the evening; and by the city lamps I could see from my window a collection of persons in the street, whose number increased till late in the night; and I heard their threats of violence to my person and destruction to my property. Towards morning, a fire occurred, and an engine passed near by, which drew after it a portion of those around the house, and attracted for a time the attention of others; and I took the opportunity to leave the house unobserved, and went to a place of concealment. While in my hiding-place, some friends took pains to ascertain whether it was prudent for me to appear again in public, and they found such a state of excitement and exasperation existing in consequence of my vote, that my life would be in danger if I was discovered. They also found that the customary routes of travel to the North were closely watched, although many believed that I had already left the city.

'Early on the morning of the second day after my unfortunate vote, I escaped from the city by an unusual route, and in disguise, and made my way to my family; and I hope now, that when the excitement has passed, I may safely return to Norfolk, at least to remain till I can settle up my affairs in that place.'

A MICHIGAN MAN DRIVEN FROM GEORGIA.

In the *Detroit Advertiser*, the following letter appears, from a correspondent in Vermontville, Michigan:

'Under date of August 19, 1856, Mr Moses C. Church, formerly a resident of this place, where his parents now live, but then being in the employ of his uncle, Harvey Hall, in Columbus, Georgia, wrote a letter to his father, which contained the following paragraph:

"Politics just now are all the go here—in fact, I never saw a community so wholly given up to it in my life. We have only two tickets—Fillmore and Buchanan, though, if there was a little more courage, and a little more concert of action, it would not be hard to get up a Fremont ticket; and though there would be no chance of his carrying the state, he would get more votes than many suppose.

"Another four years will see great changes throughout the entire South. All this talk about dissolving the Union, if Fremont is elected, is nothing but so much gas. The working, non-slaveholding mechanics, and others who are dependent upon their daily labour for their support, feel sorely the competition of non-paid labour; and they do not hesitate to say they would vote for Fremont if they had a chance. As voters, they are three to one of the slaveholders, and they are fast finding out their strength. Thinking, sober men here acknowledge that they already see the beginning of the end; and one remarked to me only last week that, in his opinion, ten years from that day would not see a slave in America. So strong is his belief, that he has disposed of all his property of that kind, and does not intend to own any more. It is a current remark here among the working-classes, that for the future those who own slaves, and have the benefit of them, may do their own watching—they will not. I claim to know what I say, as we employ a good many hands, and I know what they say."

'This paragraph was published in the *Eaton County Republican*, and some person, actuated either by a mean, low-lived spirit of mischief, or a deep-seated, infernal malignity, enclosed a half-sheet of the paper in an envelope, and forwarded it to Mr Harvey Hall. On receiving it, Mr Hall repaired, in hot haste, and full of fiery indignation, to the boarding-place of his nephew, to pour out the phial of red-hot wrath upon his head. Mr Church unhesitatingly informed his uncle that he wrote the paragraph, and that it contained his honest convictions, though he did not in the least seek to promulgate them at the South. Mr Hall then told him that if these were his sentiments, he could not entertain them at the South; and he felt it to be his duty to rid the community of his presence. He also threatened him with personal violence unless he speedily left the country. This was on Saturday. Mr Hall added further, that he must leave the first part of the next week; and if he concluded to do so, he need have no apprehension of personal violence, as he (Hall) was the only one that knew of the letter, and no measures would be taken to forcibly expel him until he should report in the matter. There were two other members of the firm which employed Mr Church. On consulting with them, though they wished his services, yet they told him he had better leave, for his uncle would surely carry his threat into execution if he did not, and the result would be riot and bloodshed. Mr Church saw that if he undertook to remain, his life would be endangered, and his wife and young child left to the tender mercies of a Georgia mob, and all heathendom, except Missouri, could not have furnished one more bloodthirsty, reckless, and unprincipled. Wisely, then, he concluded to leave; and, arranging his business as best he could, though at a sacrifice of four or five hundred dollars, did so on the next Wednesday.

'Mr Hall is a native of Vermont. He emigrated to Georgia. There he acquired wealth and slaves, and has become what he is. At his solicitation, his nephew left a lucrative situation in New York city to enter his employ; and for writing the above paragraph to his father, he is threatened with "personal violence" at the hands of the slave-driving interest of one of the cities of one of our confederate republics, unless he speedily leaves.'

DISUNION CONVENTION.

At a Disunion Convention held at Worcester, Massachusetts, January 15, 1857, the following Resolutions were submitted:

Resolved, That the meeting of the State Disunion Convention, attended by men of various parties and affinities, gives occasion for a new statement of principles, and a new platform of action.

Resolved, That the cardinal American principle is now, as always, liberty; while the prominent fact is now, as always, slavery.

Resolved, That the conflict between the principle of liberty and this fact of slavery has been the whole history of the nation for fifty years; while the only result of this conflict has thus far been to strengthen both parties, and prepare the way for a yet more desperate struggle.

Resolved, That in this emergency we can expect little or nothing from the South itself, because it is, too, sinking deeper into barbarism every year: nor from a Supreme Court, which is always ready to invent new securities for slaveholders: nor from a President elected almost solely by Southern voters: nor from a Senate which is permanently controlled by the slave-power: nor from a new House of Representatives, which, in spite of our agitation, will be more pro-slavery than the present one, though the present one has at length granted all which slavery asked: nor from political action as now conducted; for the Republican leaders and presses freely admitted, in public and private, that the election of Fremont was, politically speaking, 'the last hope of freedom;' and even could the North cast a united vote in 1860, the South has before it four years of annexation previous to that time.

Resolved, That the fundamental difference between mere political agitation and the action we propose, is this: That the one requires the acquiescence of the slave-power, and the other only its opposition.

Resolved, That the necessity for disunion is written in the whole existing character and condition of the two sections of the country —in their social organisation, education, habits, and laws—in the dangers of our white citizens in Kansas, and of our coloured ones in Boston—in the wounds of Charles Sumner, and the laurels of his assailant—and no government on earth was ever strong enough to hold together such opposing forces.

Resolved, That this movement does not seek merely disunion, but the more perfect union of the free states by the expulsion of the slave states from the confederation, in which they have ever been an element of discord, danger, and disgrace.

Resolved, That it is not probable that the ultimate severance of the Union will be an act of deliberation and discussion, but that a long period of deliberation and discussion must precede it, and this we meet to begin.

Resolved, That henceforward, instead of regarding it as an objection to any system of policy, that it will lead to a separation of the states, we will proclaim that to be the highest of all recommendations, and the grateful proof of statesmanship; and will support, politically or otherwise, such men and measures as appear to tend most to this result.

Resolved, That by the repeated confession of northern and southern statesmen, ' the existence of the Union is the chief guarantee of slavery ;' and that the despots of the whole world have everything to fear, and the slaves of the whole world everything to hope, from its destruction, and the rise of a free northern republic.

Resolved, That the sooner the separation takes place, the more peaceful it will be; but that peace or war is a secondary consideration, in view of our present perils. Slavery must be conquered, ' peaceably if we can, forcibly if we must.'

Among the more eloquent speakers at this Disunion Convention was Wendell Phillips, who took occasion to say, that, 'if high thought, high character, a noble party, a noble state, with noble impulses, be the test of government, this Union is a failure; for the character of this nation has been so barbarised in fifty years, that we must hide our faces when we compare the Senate of to-day with that over which Aaron Burr presided.' This said in New England in 1857! As has been not unusual with similar Disunion movements in the northern states, all the foregoing Resolutions expired in bluster. We give them only as a literary curiosity. Disunion, it would appear, was destined to break out in an opposite direction.

THE DRED SCOTT CASE.

This was a case brought for final decision before the supreme court of the United States. The plaintiff was a negro named Dred Scott, who, with his wife and two children, had been held as slaves by a Dr Emerson, in the state of Missouri. After the death of Emerson, Dred Scott, with his family, claimed to be free, on the ground, that they had resided for some time with their late proprietor in a free Territory—so that having, as he alleged, been free in that Territory, they could not now be held to slavery. The defendant was Emerson's administrator. The result of the litigation, which caused great excitement in the northern states, was, that Dred Scott and his family were still held to be slaves. The ultimate decision—two judges dissenting—was technically as follows:

'A negro held in slavery in one state, under the laws thereof, and taken by his master, for a temporary residence, into a state where slavery is prohibited by law, and thence into a territory acquired by treaty, where slavery is prohibited by act of congress, and afterwards returning with his master into the same slave state, and resuming his residence there, is not such a citizen of that state as may sue there in the circuit court of the United States, if by the law of that state, as repeatedly declared by its highest court in recent decisions, a negro under such circumstances is a slave; although by the law of that state at the time of his return, as settled by earlier cases, he was then a freeman; and although the new decisions be not based upon the construction of the constitution and statutes of the state, but upon the ground that the state will not enforce laws which prohibit slavery in other states or territories.'

This decision, as is believed, helped considerably to exasperate the North, and led to certain measures for nullifying the federal Fugitive Slave Law; besides contributing to promote the successful nomination of Lincoln as president.

SECESSION MOVEMENT.

The legislature of South Carolina assembled at Charleston, on the 20th of December 1860, passed the following ordinance to dissolve the union between the state and other states federated under the constitution of the United States:

'We, the people of the state of South Carolina, in Convention assembled, do declare and ordain, and it is hereby declared and ordained, that the ordinance adopted by us in Convention, on the 23d day of May, in the year of our Lord 1788, whereby the Constitution of the United States of America was ratified, and also all acts and parts of acts of the General Assembly of this state, ratifying amendments of the said Constitution, are hereby repealed, and that the union now subsisting between South Carolina and other states, under the name of the United States of America, is hereby dissolved.'

The following Declaration of Reasons for Secession, was at the same time given to the world:

'The state of South Carolina, having determined to resume a separate and equal rank among nations, deems it due to herself and the remaining United States of America, and the nations of the world, that she should declare the causes which led to the act. In 1765, that portion of the British Empire embracing Great Britain undertook to make law for the government of the American colonies. A struggle for the right of self-government ensued, which resulted, on the 4th of July 1776, in a declaration by the colonies that they are, and of right ought to be, free and independent states, and that, as free and independent states, they have full power to levy war, conclude peace, contract alliances, establish commerce, and to do such things as independent states have the right to do. They further solemnly declared that whenever any form of government becomes destructive of these ends, it is the established right of the people to alter and abolish it, and institute a new government. Deeming that the government of Great Britain had become destructive of these ends, they declared the colonies free and absolved from allegiance to the British crown, and the political connection between them and Great Britain was totally dissolved.

'The committee say the right of a state to govern itself, and the right of the people to abolish a government when it becomes destructive of the ends for which it was instituted, were expressed when the colonies separated from the mother-country and became free and independent states. The parties amending the constitution on the 17th of September 1787, were the several sovereign states.

'On the 23d of May 1788, South Carolina, by a convention of her people, assented to the amended constitution of the United States. The failure of one of the contracting parties to maintain constitutional obligations released the other. Fifteen of the northern states have deliberately refused for years to fulfil their constitutional obligations. We would refer to those states for a proof of this. When the fourth article of the constitution was adopted, the greater number of the contracting parties held slaves. The hostility of the northern states to the institution of slavery had led them to disregard their constitutional obligations. The laws of the general government have ceased to effect the objects of the constitution. Maine, New Hampshire, Vermont, Massachusetts, Connecticut, Rhode Island, New York, Pennsylvania, Illinois, Indiana, Ohio, Michigan, Wisconsin, and Iowa, have enacted laws either nullifying the constitution, or rendering useless all attempts to execute the acts of Congress. In many of those states, fugitives held to service and to labour have been claimed, but in none of them has the state government complied with the stipulation on this subject made in the constitution.

'In the formation of the federal government, each state was recognised as an equal; the right of property in slaves was recognised by giving all free persons distinct political rights; by giving them the right to represent, and burdening them with direct taxes for three-fifths of their slaves; by authorising the importation of slaves for twenty years, and by stipulating for the rendition of fugitives from labour. The ends for which this government was instituted have been defeated, and the government itself made destructive by the action of the non-slaveholding states. Those states assumed the right of deciding upon the propriety of our domestic institutions. They denied the rights of property established in fifteen states, and recognised by the constitution. They have denounced as sinful the institution of slavery; have permitted the open establishment of societies whose avowal and object are to disturb the peace and prosperity of the citizens of other states; they have encouraged and assisted thousands of our slaves to leave their homes, and those who remain have been incited by emissaries, by books and pictures, to servile insurrection. Twenty-five years this agitation has been steadily increasing, until they have secured the power of the common government. Observing the forms of the constitution, a sectional party has found within that article establishing an executive department means of subverting the constitution itself. A geographical line has been drawn across the Union, and all states north of that line have united in the elevation of a man to the high office of President of the United States whose opinions and purposes are hostile to slavery. He is to be intrusted with the administration of the common government, because it is declared that a government cannot endure permanently half slave and half free, and that the public mind must rest in the belief that slavery is in the course of ultimate extinction. The sectional combination for the subversion of the constitution has been aided in the states by elevating to citizenship persons who, by the supreme law of the land, are incapable of becoming citizens, and their votes have been used to inaugurate the new policy, hostile to the South, and destructive to its peace and safety. On the 4th of March next this party will take possession of the government. It has been announced that the South shall be excluded from the common territory; that the judicial tribunals will be made sectional; that war must be waged against slavery until it shall cease throughout the United States. The guarantees of the constitution will then no longer exist—equal rights of the states will be lost—the slaveholding states will no longer have the power of self-government or self-protection, and the federal government have become their enemy. Sectional interests and animosity will deepen the irritation, and all hope of remedy is rendered vain by the fact, that the public opinion of the North has invested the political error with the sanction of a more erroneous religious belief.

'We, therefore, the people of South Carolina, by our delegates, in Convention assembled, appealing to the Supreme Judge of the world for the rectitude of our intentions, have solemnly declared the Union heretofore existing between this state and the other states of North America dissolved, and that the state of South Carolina has resumed her position among the nations of the world as a free, sovereign, and independent state, with full power to levy war, conclude peace, contract alliances, establish commerce, and do all other acts and things which independent states may of right do; and for the support of this declaration, with a firm reliance for protection on Divine Providence, we mutually pledge each other our lives, our fortunes, and our sacred honour.'

www.ingramcontent.com/pod-product-compliance
Lightning Source LLC
Chambersburg PA
CBHW021841230426
43669CB00008B/1036